A Small Italian Life

by

Jimmy Corso
with Luanne Pendorf

authorHOUSE™

1663 Liberty Drive, Suite 200
Bloomington, Indiana 47403
(800) 839-8640
www.AuthorHouse.com

First published by AuthorHouse 03/18/05

ISBN: 1-4208-3559-9 (sc)

Library of Congress Control Number: 2005902065

Printed in the United States of America
Bloomington, Indiana

This book is printed on acid-free paper.

Photo of Jim Corso and Samson by Bill Worthen,
used by permission of Barbara Worthen.

Acknowledgements

Luanne Pendorf. The Red Dragon. With incredible presence you endured my spelling of the word parlor. You kept my spirits high, and I felt your foot behind my butt when I was discouraged and felt it wasn't worth it to keep going, especially during my Hemingway phase. Words can never express my deep gratitude for your work and relentlessness in keeping me on track writing this book. With love.

Roma Towne. My special education teacher and dear friend of fifty-five years. You dedicated your life and loyalty to teaching special education students for forty years. Your insight into my early years and family life and your encouragement throughout my early life will always be remembered.

Joanie Corso Bruso. My twin sister. Thanks for your letter. Words can never describe your "heartache" from those early years nor your beautiful soul. I love you.

Phil "Bunk" Griffin. A dear friend since the Drum and Bugle Corps days in Saranac Lake. You were the catalyst, through your website, for this book. You were the first person to read my story and you encouraged me to write it and get it published.

Shirley and Wendell Jacquith and Don Gatto. My cousins who wrote letters and helped with valuable information on my early years in the Corso side of the family.

Josephine Turco Caimano and Dolores Turco for their valuable information on the Collela side of the family. You helped me fill in the blanks.

Steve Morgan. Our friendship lasted nearly fifty years-from high school, to roommates in college, to today.Without your efforts on that July day in 1963, I would have never come to Colorado, and this story would never have been told.

Lucy Hill Duprey for all the information I forgot during our junior and senior high school years.

Duke Benz who taught me that to compete hard you must practice hard. I wish you had been my college running coach.

Bill Hakonson. Rushed me to be a TEKE, best man at my wedding, lifelong friend. Thank you for your true insight into my being during those difficult years.

Bert Thomas, biology professor, UNC. In 1963, you planted the idea for this book.

Maynard Stumper, biology professor, UNC. I am glad I had a chance to talk to you in 1990, before you passed from this earth. I can't say enough about your encouragement and help in those difficult years at Greeley.

The Science Education department at UNC for their encouragement and support during my Master's program. Especially to Dr. Sund, Dr. Crockett and Dr. Trowbridge for their support.

Marj Ireland. Who long ago passed from this earth. You taught me the true meaning of working with kids.

Jimmy Mitchell. Biology partner for many years. You taught me organizational skills.

Ben Pratt and his Arvade Driving School for giving me a chance to continue my teaching skills after retirement. The money I earned teaching those kids to drive paid for this book.

Doreena Miller for her insight and suggestions for corrections in the book.

Carl Churches. A very close friend. You know my inner soul. You taught me how to coach wrestling and I was successful because of you. I can't seem to win at the slot machines without you.

Tom Cline. A good friend and listener.

Samson, my donkey and past running partner. I miss you and hope your new owners are treating you well.

Mom and Pop for giving me life.

To my son Darren and daughter Kelley, my son-in-law Chris and daughter-in-law Maria. Words cannot express how happy I am for your success in life. Now you know why I place a strong value on reading and learning and going to church. I love you.

My grandsons Richard, Jimmy, Conner and any future grandchildren, hopefully a granddaughter I can spoil. I hope you recognize the importance of a good education. It really is a privilege to go to school and get an education.

My wife Karren. For forty years you have endured my temperamental Italian mood swings, especially while writing this book. My only fear of death is temporarily losing my family and you. I love you.

My Creator. As much as I resisted you, thank you for showing me the way.

———————————

Chapter 1

No feet, no legs, no knees. Just a stump of a beggar. I never forgot him. Maybe now, more than ever, I needed to be reminded that there were and still are people who are worse off than me. Everything is blurry and fuzzy as the shadow standing next to my bed asks me how I feel. I remember spurting out some gibberish that he didn't understand. Maybe I should have been more succinct. I feel like shit, doc!

The anesthesia was still paralyzing my body and sensory perception. I kept drifting

in and out of consciousness, one moment aware of my wife and kids, the next moment in

a dream-like state, thinking about my childhood, my dad. My mom.

Slowly, I'm walking up the stairwell and down the dimly lit hallway of the hospital. I hear the words whispering in my mind from Connie Francis' song. "Mama, until the day we're together once more, I'll live in these memories." As I enter her room I have that knot in my stomach, the one that as a kid I felt before an athletic event or when something terrible happened.

I knew that this was the end. I wouldn't be here if it wasn't. Her breathing was very slow but she wasn't suffering. She even seemed at peace, which she probably was for the first time in her life. Her dreams never fulfilled.

We were still Jimmy Boy and Joanie Girl to her. That never changed. Not even as she lay here taking her final breaths. I was still her little three year-old boy who would put his head on her lap. Comforting him with her arms around him, loving and shielding him from the world. Somehow distancing me from her fierce, fiery nature. Never letting me forget she

1

was the boss. Red welts on my arms well into my teenage years. Angry. But always loving me.

She never forgot to thank God before each meal. Most importantly she never forgot her daily prayers in front of her makeshift altar, kneeling before her icons, St. Joseph, St Anthony, St. Jude and the Blessed Mother. Prayer book and rosaries in hand. Never embarrassed, never wavering in her belief in the power of prayer. Always thank God for what you have.

Now I stand here watching her almost lifeless body, bones and muscles eaten away by cancer, ready to take her last breath, ready to be separated from her soul, ready to meet her God. I'm holding her cold hand. She whispers, Jimmy Boy why, are you crying? I want to say to her, Mom, I love you. Should it be that hard? The words never came, not even on her deathbed.

Whispering into her ear, Mom can you hear me? But there is no motion, just a lifeless body. Mom, do you remember when I was a little boy? My words drifted into silence.

Awake again, barely seeing and hearing my wife and kids. My son Darren proclaims, Dad, we finally got Samson.

Samson my donkey. My running partner.

Yeh, dad! exclaimed Kacey. Daddy's little girl was always excitable. We had to chase him halfway down the mountain, and then….

I was downstairs in the funeral parlor, picking out her casket. What a lousy feeling. We talked about what she should have. No insects should get into her casket. Then we buried her in the same cemetery as her mom and dad and all the relatives in our family. Her family and friends surrounding her grave, holding roses. Cousin Joey telling Joanie and me, Now's the time to toss the roses on her casket.

I awoke in a dark room with the family gone. The nurse is telling me it's two in the morning. I am thirsty with dry cottonmouth. I wanted something to eat but couldn't hold down any food. I wanted to go to the bathroom but couldn't. The male nurse put a catheter into my manhood to empty my bladder.

Now it's Syracuse again. Those early years, struggles, rejections, and heartache. Never knowing where I was going next, never knowing what would happen.

I wish the words would come easy. Aching to tell it for so many years. I wish I could tell it.

Why did those things happen to me? I'm feeling sorry for myself again. But then what would the phantom beggar think?

I've been here before. Hurt, angry and bitter. Only this time my injury is permanent. I close my eyes, back into a sleep, unable to move what's left of my right knee. I'm no longer able to compete, no longer able to run.

Now it's August 1963. We're driving down the freeway in an eleven year old 1952 Ford, with the student nurses in the back seat and my friend in the front seat, headed to New York City. Ironically, today is twenty years later, to the day. Mumbling, whatever happened to my friend Bunk?

———————————

Chapter 2

Subject: Old, Old Friend,
Date: Tue, Feb 15, 2001
From: "Jimmy Corso"(Paisan)
To: "Phil Griffin"

Hi Bunk,

I'm sending this against better judgment, or maybe I should say under duress. Grudgingly. I have joined the 21st century. I have a computer and I'm sending an e-mail. I don't even know what the hell the e stands for in e-mail. Being new to this contraption, I obviously don't trust it, let alone understand how it works. To me it's just another modern day contrivance. I'm a putz when it comes to these thingamagigs.

I was visiting my daughter K.C. and my son-in-law Chris in Billings, Montana and we were discussing ways of communicating with each other from Denver to Billings, via " ma bell" or postal service. Of course, being the cynic that I am, I said bring back the good old pony express. It'll be quicker.

Why write a letter or call on the phone? There's another way we can keep contact with each other.

And that would be what?

A computer.

A computer? Ooooh no. I'm not buying one of those things. I can't even figure out my T.V. set. I have four remote controls. Can't they make one remote for everything? Is that asking too much? How the heck am I going to figure out a computer when I can't even figure out a remote control?

You can do it, they said, laughing at me as if I was some kind of a little boy. Why don't you "get with it" and come into the new century! Hint dad! It's the new way of communicating.

What happened to the old way? I growled. Like using a t e l e p h o n e? I said slowly to try and emphasize my point of view.

Dad! It's better and cheaper than the telephone. You can use what they call an e-mail.

What the hell is an e-mail?

Think typewriter, dad. With letters and numbers located in the same position as that typewriter you used in the old days?

Hey, you're a little loose with the tongue, young lady. I'm not that old. Besides, there was nothing wrong with those old typewriters. The hunt and peck method I used with those old typewriters got me through a lot papers in college.

Yes, dad, that was true for you, especially the hunt and peck method (laughing), but didn't you also have to use two sheets of paper with a carbon paper in-between them and when you made a mistake you had to erase the word on the first copy as well as the second? And how many mistakes did you have to erase on those carbons?

Well, Bunk, to get to the meat of the story, and to appease my kids, right then I went to COSTCO and bought a computer. It was cheaper in Montana, because they have no sales tax. Hooray for Montana. Some governments get it right, don't they?

Chris, with an electrical engineering degree, had to hook it up for me the following weekend when they came to Arvada. But by then it wasn't just the computer. There was also a printer, and a scanner. Then I had to go to the local school's Internet services and purchase a CD to hook it up to the Internet. From there I had to get a teacher friend to help me with all the Windows, Netscape, and all that stuff. Ah...but I wasn't through. Then I had to get something called a Norton Antivirus disk. Being a biology teacher, I asked how the heck can a computer get a virus? Viruses go with colds, not computers! I could have made three months of long distance calls for the time and money this has already cost me.

Welcome to the new technology in the 21st Century.

And, Bunk, I now have to be concerned about spam e-mail. I get 80 e-mails a day either about mortgage payments, or drugs to make my reproductive organ firmer, plus implants to make it stronger, faster, thicker, wider, and longer than an elephant's trunk.

I'm not sure it's worth it. You're probably wondering how I found your e-mail address. It wasn't easy, at least not for me. Once, I got past turning on the computer, my problems began.

I made a good old-fashioned phone call to Steve Morgan. He told me you had a website. After much hide and seek and going through Yahoo, and I don't know what, I finally hit all the correct letters and hocus-pocus. Bingo! There was your web site, Bunk's Mountain Home Companion, in Saranac Lake, New York. And yes, the hunt and peck method still works well.

It's been 38 years. Holy smokes! Where has all the time gone? What have you been doing since 1963? That was the last time I saw you. We were headed down the freeway in my dad's 52 Ford, taking Carol, Judy and Cindy from the Alpine Lodge to catch a plane from New York City to Michigan. After the girls left that night, we headed to Times Square. We talked and shook hands with the great drummer Gene Krupa. Do you remember what happened next? The clutch broke and we were stranded right in the heart of Times Square? We pushed the car off the street to the curb, but it was so late at night we decided to sleep in the car, with New York's finest waking us up at three in the morning telling us to beat it. But officer, the clutch is broken, we can't drive the car. That's not our problem, son. You can stay till daylight, then move it. Getting to a garage to tow and fixing the clutch cost seventy dollars, and I still owe you ten bucks for helping with the bill. I'll gladly pay now by sending you a case from the brewery that produces beer from the finest and purest Rocky Mountain Spring water.

Married? Any family? How is your brother Bob and Diane, my old girlfriend he married? And what has happened to the old gang? Are any of them still in town? I am ashamed to admit that I have forgotten some of their nicknames. But then we did have lots of guys and gals in that gang.

Hey, you've got a great website. I like your page that has information on current news in the tri-lake area (Lake Placid, Tupper Lake and Saranac Lake), and your gallery site with photos of current and past graduates from the high school, and their comments about their favorite memories in Saranac. Swimming in Crescent Lake, really brought back some great memories for me, especially when we went skinny-dipping. Brrr...that water was sure cold. I miss those days and our little village in the heart of the Adirondack Mountains.

I'm looking forward to hearing from you.

Jimmy Corso (aka Paisan).

Reply: Old, Old, Friend
Date: Web. Feb. 16, 2001
From: "Phil Griffin"
To: "Jimmy Corso"

Hey Jimmy, or should I say, Paisan,

This is great. The main reason I created this site five or six years ago was to reunite old friends. Once in a while, I am pleasantly surprised by hearing from some of my old friends.

It was a double surprise today. I heard from Sandy Richardson this morning. It makes the work on the page worth it when things like this happen. A lot of Saranac Lakers have been reunited here, and it always makes me feel good. It's even better when it happens to me.

I'm married and have two daughters and a grandson, C.J. I work at the local state hospital. I always wanted to be a journalist, but as you are well aware things don't always work out the way we want to in life.

When my brother Bob and I talk about the good old days, and they were, your name always comes up. Sometimes I wonder how we survived. You mentioned nicknames. I will try to think of as many as possible. See how many you can remember. Ostrich, Elephant, Goat, Barfly, Rocky, Skeeter, Massacar, Tiny, and Spook (who was always telling us to "buy and go, purchase and leave"). Toilet lips, as you might remember, died in a car accident in 1962. Skeeter died in 1963, also in a car accident. Eskimo, also known as Muk-luk, died a few years ago in New York City. And of course you, Paisan, the friendly Wop. I sometimes think I should start an extra page named after us called "The Arcade Gang".

You know, we really had quite a crew when you stop to think of it. Even the most boring nights had a lot of amusement value. Whenever I see "American Graffiti" I think of our gang as a small town version of what was going on at that time in Los Angeles or wherever that story took place.

When I see kids hanging out today I often think of our gang. We must have seemed like punks to the adults then. I don't think we were that bad though. (Well, once in a while we did walk the edge).

Well, once again, great to hear from you. Keep in touch and keep visiting the page. Now that I know I have my old buddies are out there it will be an inspiration to me. And yes, I'll gladly accept a case from the Rocky Mountain pure spring waters. Thanks for thinking of me.

Bunk.

Subject: Jimmy's Story
Date: Feb 17, 2001
From: "Jimmy Corso"
To: "Phil Griffin"

Hi Bunk,

I found your e-mail very interesting. For many years I've wanted to write a book about my own experiences before I arrived in Saranac Lake.

Nobody knows the story, except my cousins back East and Roma Towne, my special education teacher. In fact, I've never even told Karren and the kids. I never told anyone out of shame and embarrassment. But if it's okay with you I'd like to tell you the story via, uhm… this e-mail that I don't trust.

My first fifteen years set the stage for my later life. Let me know what you think. I value your opinion. Is it worth a book, or just a pile of junk for the trash, a pipe dream that will never be fulfilled?

My sister had already been born, twenty minutes earlier. I didn't want to come out. And why should I? Inside, I'm cozy, secure, and everything is nice and fuzzy warm. Everything is provided for me: breathing, food, waste removal, and a place to sleep. Outside it's cold, hostile. Soon I'm one minute old in the new world, the real world.

Myth: I was born retarded and have an I.Q. of 70.

Reality: Life is not fair. We all know that. If it was, Bunk, you would have been that journalist and I would have been Jay Leno or David Letterman. My fantasy, expounding with sarcastic humor about people, places and things.

Even if life isn't exactly fair, most of us do have choices about our life, and they start at an early age. Either we pout about our fate or existence or we pick ourselves up by the "old bootstraps" and make something of our lives. I chose to do the latter.

The school psychologist said I couldn't make it in a regular class, that I was too slow. The nuns said I couldn't make it in regular class, that I was too slow. If it wasn't the teachers, it was administrators, or counselors who said I couldn't achieve my goals, that I was too slow. Hell, even my parents doubted my learning abilities.

My story is not "rags to riches". Mine is out to in. How I got <u>out</u> of special education and <u>into</u> the regular classroom. I made it, Bunk, despite my family life, despite the number of moves and schools in my life. What I did was suck it up and tough it out--despite all the despites.

Paisan

8

Hey Paisan,

The system really can screw up a young life. If you knock a kid down often enough they eventually will fit themselves into the mold that you've created for them.

I hope you write that book. It will be a great benefit to you just to get it off your chest. It would also be good to share your feelings with your family. Sometimes we carry around guilt feelings because we think we could have somehow prevented things from happening. Even things that happened at an early age. I'm nowhere near being a writer, but I could help with the outline, etc. if you want.

Later, Bunk

———————————

Chapter 3

To understand my six years in special education, you'll need to understand my early years in an Italian American family.

Grandpa Colella was born in Abruzzi, Italy. No one knows where grandma Colella was born. My Mom, Lena (Carmella), was born in 1919, in Syracuse, New York, one of thirteen children born to grandma and grandpa Colella. She was a sixth grade drop out who could speak fluent Italian and English. She was a tea totaler, never drank or smoked, very high-strung person, but quiet and shy. Most times she did not like being in large groups of people, even within the family. She was very over-protective, a helicopter parent. Sometimes she was very strict, but she was also very loving, sensitive and compassionate. She was a devout Catholic, unwavering in her belief in God, and she went to church and received communion every Sunday. No matter where we lived, she would make a small altar with a statue of the blessed mother draped in rosaries, kneeling in front of a statue of Joseph and Jesus. Every day she was on her knees with her prayer book and rosaries, praying.

I don't think she committed a sin in her life. She never worked until 1965, when she was 46 years old. She worked for the state of New York as an aide taking care of invalids, bathing and cleaning them. I asked her how she could do that type of work.

It's God's will.

Grandpa Corso was born in Palermo, Italy. No one knows where grandma Corso was born. In 1916, in Syracuse, New York, my Pop, Jim, who they called Murphy, was born, one of ten children born to grandpa and grandma Corso. He never had any self-discipline, never worried about anything and was economically dysfunctional. He had a hard time paying his bills because he threw his money away on gambling and booze. He was always in debt because he didn't believe in saving money. He never had a savings account his entire life.

We need money now. The future will take care of itself.

But Pop would give a person the shirt off his back. He went bankrupt twice in his life, and went through AA twice. Hell raiser, always liked to be with the guys to play cards, bowl and drink. Flew by the seat of his pants. Most of all, he always avoided his problems, which he created, by moving to a new job or a new location. But he was smart, a fast learner, a master craftsman, and a "jack of all trades". Great hands. From plumbing, to carpentry to electrical work, windows, furnaces, cement. He could do it all.

Was Pop wild? I asked grandma, half-joking, and half-serious at one of our family reunions. In her broken English she told me this true but sad story.

At 2:30 in the morning, grandpa and I were waked up by the phone. It was a man from the police station saying your papa was in a terrible car accident. But grandpa and I didn't want to go because we were tired of his ways. So we sent Uncle Gus and Uncle Sam.

Your dad, Murphy was driving, interrupted Uncle Gus, taking a sip of his soda. His date was next to him in the front seat. His best friend and his date were in the back seat. I remember walking into the station and your dad was sitting down on a bench covering his face, crying. Mumbling something about I killed him! I killed him!

What happened, Murphy? I said to him.

We had a few drinks, we were driving fast, and we came on this blind corner. It was dark, with no street or traffic lights, not even a stop sign. I tried to brake but it was too late. We hit the other car head on. It killed Johnny.

Pop never forgot about the accident. It hunted him the rest of his life.

Then there was his marriage to Mom in 1937. I never could figure out this relationship. I often wondered how two such opposite people connected.

I never bothered to ask how they got together until many years later at another family reunion. Those reunions. I learned so much about the dark side of the family.

Joanie and I were sitting at the dinner table with our cousins Donnie and Shirley, and with Mom and Pop. The rest of the family was in the parlor discussing politics. When our conversation centered on dating, I finally had my opportunity to ask them how they met.

With her legs crossed and arms folded, Mom said, Well, Jimmy, we dated for several months, and then we got married.

Just several months? I said laughing, shoving a piece of calamari into my mouth.

This is no joke, said Mom.

I was at a dance with my fiancé, said Pop.

Was she Italian, Uncle Murph?

Yes, she was, Shirley. Anyways, we had a bad argument. I got mad, called off the wedding and walked off the dance floor.

That sounds like you, Uncle Murph, said Donnie, laughing and taking a sip of wine.

So, a short time later I saw your mother talking with some of her friends. I wanted to make my ex-fiancé jealous, so I walked over to your mom and asked her to dance.

It must have been opposites attract, huh dad?

Why's that, Jimmy?

Look at you two. You're 5'7" and weigh 195 pounds and Mom's 4'10" and weighs 90 pounds.

We courted for about three months. One night I just asked your mom to marry me.

After three months! If Joanie and I did that you'd kill us.

Poppycock, (an unusual word from a macho Italian) said Pop. We wouldn't have said anything.

Oh, yes you would have! blurted Joanie, giving Pop a friendly dirty look. We'd have never heard the end of it. We'd get all kinds of lectures. Why'd you want to get married so young? You hardly know each other. You got your whole life ahead of you. Date other guys. There's other fish in the sea. Oh, yeh, you definitely would have! And mom, how could you do that?

Times were different in those days, Joanie.

But, three months, that's ridiculous.

So what happened? I mumbled impatiently, eating another piece of Calamari.

I'll tell you exactly what happened, said Pop, taking a swallow of his wine. Carmella, I said to her, even though I knew she hated that name, let's get married.

Are you crazy? We've known each other only three months.

So, what difference does that make?

We better wait, Murph. We hardly know each other.

What's there to know? I know you're a virgin. What's the problem? We've known each other long enough.

But what will our folks say? Our families? Our friends?

The hell with them! We're getting married, not them.

I'm not sure this is the best thing to do. What about work? Where will we live? And what about money?

The hell with the money! Besides, I can do anything. I can do carpentry, plumbing, anything. We can live on Seymour Street with my folks.

No! I don't what to live with anybody, especially relatives.

Then let's elope and not tell anyone. Nobody needs to know. When we're ready we can tell everybody.

I want to get married in a church and by a priest and papa walking me down the aisle on a white carpet with a little girl in front of us throwing flowers, with a maid of honor and bridesmaid.

We can get married by a judge or whatever. Later, we can get it blessed by a priest. Plus everything else you want. We just can't have it right now. What do you say, babe?

So…we got married. He took another swallow of wine.

I could see that Mom had a distant look in her eyes, maybe sorrow. I'm not sure what it meant, and I didn't ask.

We got married on March 19, 1937. I had just tuned 18. Dad was 21.

When did you tell the families?

Not for three years.

Three years! Several of us said at the same time, and Joanie and I looked at each other in amazement.

How could you do that and not have the families know you were married?

It wasn't easy, Joanie, said Pop laughing.

No, said Mom in her usual quiet, submissive manner.

How did you get together for sex? I asked.

Well………Pop was laughing.

That's none of your business, Jimmy!

That's none of your business, Jimmy. I sarcastically mocked Mom, in baby talk. If looks could kill, I would have been dead.

We lived with our families and saw each other on the weekends. And there were times that we went away for couple of days.

To have sex! I said, with all of us laughing except Mom, who gave me another dirty look.

Nobody suspected anything. We were together for a long time so I don't think anyone cared.

It was an impulsive move by Mom. But not for Pop. He was impulsive. The sad part was that Mom never was married in the church, no priest, no petals, no bridesmaid, no guests, or wedding reception or honeymoon. The wedding that Mom always wanted, in a church, by a priest, she never got.

After they told the families they were married, they lived on Seymour Street. The house was much better than Grandma and Grandpa Colella's house on Kingsley Place, which was a cold, drafty, smelly, broken down dump, a pigsty. Definitely not the New York Hilton.

The house on Seymour Street was large. It actually was four small apartments. Each apartment had an Aunt and Uncle living in it. At one time or another most of the family lived in one of those apartments. One part of the family would move out and another one would move in. With as many as fifteen living in the house, no one really had any privacy. They were fortunate, though, because they had plumbing at a time when only fifty percent of the homes in America had indoor plumbing. Mom, Pop, Joanie and I lived in that house for nine years. That house is still there.

Paisan

Chapter 4

Hey Paisano,

My brother Bob remembers one time when he and your dad were working for the lumber company and Bob forgot his lunch. Your dad saw that he didn't have any lunch or money with him and called him over to sit down with him and gave him some of his lunch. Bob never forgot that. You said that your folks didn't tell anyone for three years. That's a long time to keep that kind of a secret. Why did they finally decide to tell everyone? Bunk

---

Yep, Bunk, it was a long time to keep that kind of a secret. In fact, my cousin Shirley asked about that at the reunion.

Hey, Uncle Murph. How come you finally decided to tell the family that you and Aunt Lena were married?

I got pregnant, Shirley.

At least we know it wasn't a shotgun wedding, Aunt Lena.

I wasn't like that, Donnie. And you know that.

We're just teasing you, Aunt Lena.

Anyways, your mom was getting sick in the morning and we suspected that she might be pregnant, so I took her to the doctor.

Hey, Aunt Lena, why didn't you ever learn how to drive?

I don't like driving, Shirley. I can't get everything together.

What's everything?

She can't coordinate the clutch and shift gears at the same time, said Pop.

And she doesn't know that when there is a car in front of you, you need to. . . um…put your foot on the brake pedal, I said laughing.

I've tried teaching her, but I don't have the patience said Pop. Also, she's too nervous. When she sees the other cars coming towards her on the other side of the road, she thinks they are going to come into her lane and crash into her.

I just don't like driving. I get too scared.

Hey, someone please pass the calamari.

How many of those are you going to eat, Jimmy?

I don't know. Why? Is somebody counting?

Do you guys want to hear the rest of the story or not?

Yes, Uncle Murph.

Lena was in the doctor's office a long time.

Or, what seemed like a long time to your dad. You know your dad. If he has to wait more than ten minutes for anything, then it's a long time. If he is in the car then he beeps his horn for me to hurry up. I walked out of the doctor's office and told your dad. I'm pregnant.

What did I tell you? That shouldn't come as a surprise. You've been sick every morning.

He thinks the baby will be born in January.

The next few months I got big and had a hard time carrying the extra weight.

Pop interrupted. I took mom back to the doctor's in July.

You're awful big. Do you think it could be twins? I bet my last dollar they will be born around the first week of December.

What makes you think it will be December? The doctor doesn't even know that!

Look how huge you are. You haven't been pregnant that long.

That's because I am tiny and it makes me look larger.

We'll see in a few months, babe.

On our next visit to the doctor's mom came out of the doctor's and told me, guess what?

What?

It's twins!

What did I tell you, babe?

But, the doctor still thinks it will be January.

It's December, babe. Wait and see.

That Thanksgiving weekend we were sitting around the table and Mom was touching her side.

What's the matter, Lena?

Just having some stomach pains.

Are you sure it's not contractions?

If they are, they aren't very painful.

By Monday, it was a different story. Those stomach pains were now severe contractions. They weren't close, but she was definitely having contractions. The next morning I got a call to go to Crouse Irving Hospital. Mom was in labor.

At 10:00 the doctor came out into the waiting room and told me that I had a six pound, 17 inches baby girl. But, the other baby wasn't born yet and we didn't know if it was a boy or a girl.

I guess I didn't want to come out. Maybe I knew what was in store for me. Everyone laughed at my little joke.

Twenty minutes later the doctor came back out and tells me I have a six pound, 10 ounce, 18 inches boy. I was right. It was December 1, 1940.

But what you guys didn't know, and dad won't tell anyone, was that you and Joanie were premature. I was only eight months pregnant.

Although historically 1940 was an interesting year, none of it really affected Joanie and me. President Roosevelt was re-elected to his third term. "Because of You" was one of the top songs of the year and big bands dominated the music scene with such songs as "Moonlight Serenade" by Glenn Miller, "Jumpin' at the Woodside" by Count Basie, and "Solitude" by Duke Ellington. Then there were Benny Goodman, Tommy Dorsey and Hoagie Carmichael who sang his great song, "Stardust". The RCA labs demonstrated the electron microscope. The Rockefeller Institute discovered the RH factor in blood. M & M candy was produced for the U.S. military. Fifty-five percent of the homes had indoor plumbing. A three bed room home cost 3, 925 dollars, a new Ford 700 dollars, and half a gallon of milk 52 cents. A gallon of gas was 18 cents. Minimum wage was 43 cents per hour. The average income was 2, 310 dollars.

A week later Mom was allowed to come home. Then, new mothers stayed in the hospitals a long time and fathers were not allowed in the delivery room. A far contrast to today's standards, wouldn't you say, Bunk?

We were the center of attention. We had to be. We had to be fed, changed, clothed and definitely demanded much time and care. All this started to wear on Mom. She was already physically weak, and Pop said her mental condition was starting to become a problem.

As Joanie and I were growing, crawling and getting into things, the world scene got worse. Hitler had already invaded Poland, and his influence in Germany was very strong. A year after we were born the world was at war. A year and half later, in the summer of 1942, our family journeys began.

Chapter 5

To piece together those early years I called my oldest cousin Shirley who was our babysitter, especially after the war started.

What I remember, Jimmy, is that in the summer of 1942, your mom and dad moved to Oswego. Your dad was in some kind of a business with Uncle Gus. Uncle Gus's brother-in-law was part owner of a bar and grill in Oswego. Your mom and dad rented the upstairs apartment. I enjoyed babysitting you and Joanie, which I did quite often. By the way, do you remember everybody in the family calling you Jimmy Boy and Joanie Girl? Nobody knew why.

Yesssss. Laughing. So what else can you tell me?

One day that summer I came to Oswego with my mom and dad to baby-sit so all the adults could go out together. You and Joanie were taking a nap. At least I thought you were taking a nap. I was in the kitchen reading a magazine, and the phone rings.

Is Lena there?

No, this is Shirley, her niece. I'm babysitting the twins.

Well, Shirley, the twins are running on top of the roof.

What?!

Yes. And they're naked!

I went up to the upstairs bedroom and looked out the window. There you were, Jimmy, peeing on the roof and Joanie was running up and down from one level of the roof to the next. I can remember yelling, Hey, you two get in here! What do you two think you are doing? Are you crazy? You can kill yourselves! Now get in here! Now!

Damn! Jimmy, I was really mad. I can laugh about it now, but not then. You guys could have seriously hurt yourselves. And thank God you didn't.

About a year later you moved back to Syracuse on Seymour Street. Your mom was getting worse mentally and so was the war. Your dad was working at the steel mill then. Although your dad was 26 at that time, he was still home. The service was taking younger boys.

Later that summer I was babysitting and again I thought you two were taking a nap. This time you were living upstairs in the front apartment on Seymour Street. I was downstairs talking to grandma. In fact, and I bet you didn't know this, because we had so few beds, I had to share the same bed with grandma for several years. Do you know what's it like sleeping in the same bed with your grandma? I didn't like it and it certainly wasn't funny. Grandma and I were talking when we heard a "thud" on the floor. We immediately went upstairs to see what happened. When we opened the door, what a sight.

Matti! Cried out grandma. Crazy kids!

I poked my head in the door, "Oh my God." I was laughing. You and Joanie had somehow managed to get two large Crisco cans from the pantry, had made snowballs and then thrown them all over the floor and walls, ruining the wallpaper.

Or how about the day you and Joanie took off and followed the fire truck on Seymour Street? You must have been about five or six years old. Your mom realized you were not in the front yard and of course she panicked. She came running into the house yelling to your dad. The twins are gone! I've looked in front and back and can't find them!

Everything will be all right. Let's go down the street. They're probably at one of the neighbors' houses.

A neighbor saw us. Are you looking for the twins?

Yes! Lena said in a panicked voice.

I just saw them following the fire truck. It's just around the corner.

The minute we saw you, you and Joanie tried to hide from us. Your mom scolded you so bad that even I was afraid to go near her.

I don't remember running on top of the roof, but I do remember getting a butt warming from Mom for following the fire truck.

———————————

Chapter 6

I remember Pop telling me about that bar Uncle Gus' relative had in Oswego. It was years later, out here in Arvada, when we were sitting at the kitchen table in his apartment. I asked him what happened to that bar in Oswego.

Why do you want to know about that, Jimmy? Pop asked.

I want to write a book.

A book? He looked at me in a very quizzical way. About what?

My six years in special education. Remember, the school psychologists said I was retarded because I scored a 70 on their test?

What's the bar got to do with the story?

I don't know. I was thinking about those early years and the bar popped into my head. You're 81 years old Pop. I need as much information as you can give me. You're not going to live forever.

Pop walked over to the closet and brought out a gallon of Paisano wine and poured himself a glass of wine.

Do you want some wine?

No. It's too early in the day, plus it makes me sleepy. I have to drive home.

It was called Signeralli's and was owned by Uncle Gus's brother-in-law, Jim.

I remember going there, Pop, when I was eight or nine.

They got killed. Not missing a beat he continued talking. But the bar had to be closed in the late 40's. Jim and one his friends were out partying one night and got into a car accident. They were traveling so fast that somehow their car hit a large bump on the side of the road, flew in the air and hit the middle of a telephone pole. Killed both of them. Shortly after that we moved back to Syracuse. It was the summer of 42 and mom was starting to have a hard time emotionally. You know mom had two mental breakdowns when you and Joanie were growing up. Eventually they sent her to a sanitarium. She had been getting worse, but I didn't really know about it until I came home one night and I couldn't find her.

Hearing some murmurs in the bathroom, I opened the door and found her sitting on the floor crying.

What's wrong, babe?

Nothing.

Then why are you curled up on the floor crying?

I don't know.

Did ma help you with the kids today?

Just a little. Besides, you know how your mom is. I'm sorry I ever agreed to live here. It's been nothing but problems.

Why's that? Ma is just trying to help.

Help me do what! When I try to punish the kids I get criticized. I shouldn't do this and shouldn't do that. That's no way to raise your kids.

We'll make the best of it and then I'll try to get our own apartment. Right now get up off the floor and clean up. Everyone will be coming home soon.

According to the newspapers the war was as bad as ever. Things were rationed, food, gas, clothing.

Crucible steel mill. I worked ten-hour days. Because I was 27, I was at the tail end of being drafted, but that didn't mean the service wouldn't take me.

When I came home from work I was too tired to do anything with you and Joanie, and your Mom was exhausted from taking care of you two all day.

The war was taking a toll on everyone, even if they were not in the service. People were making all kinds of sacrifices. And then grandpa was sick too. I suppose carrying that wine jug around the house all day was wearing him out.

Mom kept getting worse. A week later I came home from work and called for her. When she didn't answer I went to the kitchen and saw grandma cooking.

Where's Lena?

She's in the cellar.

Cellar? What is she doing down there?

I think you need to get her some help. I asked her to come upstairs but she didn't say anything. She's been coughing. I think she's coming down with a cold.

Where are the twins?

21

In the parlor.

I found your Mom sitting on the floor of the cellar with her knees bent to her chest, crying.

Lena, are you okay?

I'm fine! Leave me alone! Just go away!

The next day I called Dr. Grant, our family doctor.

I told him mom had been acting very strange. Twice I've come home from work and found her in the bathroom and then the cellar, sitting on the floor with her knees to her chest, crying. Sometimes, she doesn't even remember talking to me.

How long had this been going on, Jim?

Ever since the twins were born, she started acting funny.

What do you mean funny?

Strange. At times she doesn't want to be near anyone in the family, and she just starts crying and not remembering doing things or talking to me.

Dr. Grant talked to mom alone for about a half hour. Then he said Lena needs help. I think she is having a nervous breakdown.

A nervous breakdown? How could that happen?

I don't know, Jim. We're not sure how these things happen. It could be pressure from everyday things. Raising the twins, the war. Who knows? Lena is a very sensitive and nervous person. I think things affect her personally, especially relationships with her family. I also notice she has a dry cough and a slight temperature. How long has she had this cough?

I don't know. On and off, I guess. I haven't paid much attention to it. Ma said she was coughing a lot last week. We thought it was just a cold.

I want to run a series of tests on her. Take her to the Onondaga clinic tomorrow.

What kind of tests?

I have a hunch, Jim

Hunch about what?

Tuberculosis.

Tuberculosis? You think she has TB?

She has the symptoms. I would like to take an x-ray of her lungs and see if we can detect any spots of bacterium. We'll need to do a test to check her sputum, what we call spit and a skin test. It will take a few days to get the results.

How did she get this?

I'm not sure. We used to think that it was transmitted by contaminated food or milk, but new research has shown us that the germs that caused the infection are breathed in by dust and air. People who have T.B. spread the germs into the air by coughing. Once the germs are air-borne, they can be inhaled into the body, spread to the lungs.

Then why don't any of us have it?

Maybe you can resist it better than she can. The stress of carrying both the kids and her mental condition. Lena is a very nervous person. All combined, these weaken her system. If she does have TB, we'll need to take measures to protect everyone in the family. Also, Jim, she might have to go to a sanitarium for a complete recovery. I'll call you in a few days. In the meantime I will contact a doctor I know who specializes in mental conditions and see if he will talk to Lena.

On top of this news from about Mom, came the word that the services were now drafting older men. It was looking more like Pop would have to go.

When Pop told Mom he could be drafted soon, he said he was going to sign up.

It's that or be drafted by the Army. I want to enlist in the Navy. Besides, Joey's in the Navy, maybe I'll get a chance to see him someplace.

When is this going to happen?

February. But I'll wait and see what the doctor has to say about you.

This was the start of a long mental and physical condition that would last until the day Mom died. It's also when grandma and grandpa Corso took care of Joanie and me and when we started acting like wild animals in a cage.

Pop remembered a lot of this. He had an amazing memory for facts and figures, especially in the later years of his life. He continued his story. One day Grandma and I were in the parlor when she answered the phone.

Is Jim there, Theresa? This is Jim Grant.

Yes, un momento.

Jim, it's Jim Grant.

Yep.

Jim, I got back the results. Lena has tuberculosis. You'll need to bring her here so we can discuss some things you need to do for sanitary reasons. Can you bring Lena to the office at 9:00 in the morning?

We'll be there. Thanks.

The next day Mom and Pop listened quietly as Dr. Grant gave them specific instructions to follow at home.

Do not drink out of the same cup or glasses. Wash all dishes, glasses, cups and clothes, pillowcases and sheets, several times a week. Take extra precautions about kissing. You do not want to spread the germs. But, most of all, she will need plenty of rest.

Also, I have been in contact with the doctor that evaluated Lena. She is on the verge of a nervous breakdown and is becoming very depressed. Her short memory losses are not uncommon for people in her condition. She will need help as soon as possible. Right now the doctor and I have agreed the best solution would be to send her to a sanitarium in Raybrook, New York. It is an excellent place for her to get help. It is located up north in the Adirondack Mountains, a few miles from Lake Placid, where they held the 1932 winter Olympics. There she can get the rest she needs. Maybe that will also help her depression.

How much will it cost?

I know you don't have much money, so I talked to the people at the sanitarium. They have help for special cases like you. You'll need to pay only the minimum. It won't be much. Are you still working in the steel mill?

Yes, but I've enlisted in the Navy and will be leaving in January. I don't want to be drafted.

That's only a couple of months away. She won't be home for the holidays. Who will take care of the twins?

My ma and pa.

That's going to be hard on everyone, including the twins.

Yeh, but there's nothing we can do about it. Where do we go from here?

We'll need to make arrangements for her at the sanitarium. She will be under the care of a Dr. Trudeau. His dad had TB and was convinced there needed to be a place to help people who contracted this disease. He established the sanitarium in the late 1880's. This should be an excellent place for her. Do you have any questions Jim?

Nope.

Remember about keeping everything clean. I'll contact you in a few days about taking her up north.

Pop took a big swallow of wine, burped, wiped his mouth with his sleeve, and not missing a beat, he continued his story. A few days later, Dr. Grant called back saying he was coming to the house to see us.

How can you remember all of this, Pop?

I don't know. It seems like yesterday. It's all gone by too fast.

I was in the parlor drinking a glass of wine when Dr. Grant showed up. Doctors made house calls in those days. Pop laughed. He was always taking care of you and Joanie, especially you, because you always were sick with bronchitis.

Hmm. Guess I don't have any T-cells.

Any what?

Nothing Pop. An inside joke I have with my immune system.

Doc Grant made arrangements for mom to check into the sanitarium at Raybrook in January. The doctors felt it would be best for her to be home for the holidays with the family. After Christmas, I took mom to the sanitarium where she stayed until the end of the year.

As I watched Pop, he finished his glass of Paisano wine and then poured himself another. His eyes were watery with a distant glaze as he stared out the window. He missed Mom, never adjusted to her death. He was lost, his spirit broken.

Then he continued. A few days later we got together for our usual Sunday dinner. We pushed several tables together and there was homemade bread, pasta, sausages, meatballs, cannoli, salads, wine and coffee.

And all during dinner we argued, because Jimmy, remember, we're an Italian family, in 1943, arguing about politics, economy, religion, the mafia, and, of course, God's part in the war.

The men would argue. The women rarely took part. Our discussions were very heated, but we talked with our hands, not with our fists, and we never had anything in a violin case. With that smirk on his face, I couldn't tell if he was joking or being cynical because Pop was always sensitive about stereotyping Italians, especially when it came to the Mafia.

Another swig of wine. The fact was, Jimmy, when the war first broke out, Italy was on the side of Japan.

I know Pop, I'm aware of my American History.

Anyways, some people never forgave the Italians. As a matter of fact, many Italians weren't accepted when they first came here. That's why some of them changed their last names to non-Italian ones. But people forgot how many of us served in the war. And a few were even interned in camps like they did the Japanese Americans. I think Uncle Billy was at Normandy on D-day. We did our part for this country, despite what people thought about us before and after the war.

Then all of a sudden he shifted topics and said, that was also the night that you had your accident and burned your face.

What accident? I don't remember any accident.

Of course you wouldn't, you were only three.

Why didn't you or Mom tell me about this before?

I guess we never thought about it.

Anyways, when we finished the main meal, the women cleared all the dishes from the table and then served cannoli and a pot of coffee. This time when you saw the cannoli, you knocked over the coffee pot to get one. The coffee pot crashed on the table spilling hot coffee all over your face. All hell broke loose with mom and you hysterical and crying. Aunt

Fran rushed to get butter to put on your face and Grandma yelled, Call the doctor! When we got to the hospital the doctor on duty was already waiting for us at the emergency room. I still laugh about this. He grabbed you, and at the same time said to mom and me, you two wait here, we can't have three hysterical people in the room. Jimmy will be fine. After what seemed like a long time the doctor finally came out of the emergency room holding you. Your face was covered with some special thick cream that had to be put on every day for weeks until your face looked good again. I don't know what he used, but you never had any lasting scars.

Pop finished his glass of wine and put it down hard on the table, wiped his face with his sleeve, went to the closet and got another half-gallon jug of wine, and poured himself another glass.

So, he continued, the next few months were pretty bad. I enlisted in the Navy and was gonna be leaving for Norfolk, Virginia the first of the year. I took mom to the sanitarium in Raybrook. But she was so upset about me going into the Navy and her having to go into the sanitarium, everything just got worse.

Who will take care of the kids?

We've already been over that, Lena. Ma and Pa will take care of them. Gus and Sam will be around to help out. They won't be drafted. They're too old. Everybody will help out.

What about the money? Where are we going to get money to pay the bills for the sanitarium?

Don't worry about the bills! I've already worked that out with the doctors. You get better. Leave the worrying to me. God will work it out.

This was pretty hypocritical of Pop. He never worried about anything. He did what he wanted to do in life, when he wanted to do it. He never worried about the consequences. Then he would top it off with his famous saying: God will work it out. That way he never had to be responsible for his actions. And when the results were bad, and they often were, he could avoid his problems by moving to a new house or job or town.

Like I did all my life, I avoided challenging him about his hypocrisy. I didn't show my feelings because I knew he would defend his actions, ultimately resulting in another argument. I learned that the best way to avoid conflicts was to keep quiet and not say anything, even if it meant keeping things inside me, always opting for peace and quiet.

In January of '44, I was in the Navy and Mom in the sanitarium. Grandma and Grandpa now had the responsibility of taking care of you and Joanie, a huge responsibility for Grandma who was 60, and Grandpa who was nearly 75.

Pop continued with the story, but not before pouring another glass of wine. Then I watched this once powerful man, grab his walker and slowly shuffle to the bathroom. At two hundred and twenty-five pounds, even riddled with osteoporosis, his body could still hold a lot of wine.

I came home during the summer of '44 for a week to see Mom. But before I saw her, I had to talk to Dr.Trudeau. I remember it was a long drive up there with those winding roads. There was the usual small talk about the Navy and the war. Then Dr. Trudeau gave me the news.

Lena has been through a rough time since you left for the service. She had made some progress against her TB, but emotionally she has had a very difficult time. She is very depressed and lonely. She goes through weeks of not remembering things. This must have been happening for some time. It could be the combination of many factors: the physical stress of having the twins and now not being able to see them. It could be the war and you being in the service. All of this has been building up inside of her. We can treat the TB, but we are not experts with the mind. You are going to have to get some expert help for her. But for right now we would like to keep her here.

How much longer?

She might be able to go home in December. You can see her for a while. It will be good for both of you.

She and I talked for a while, but then I drove back to Syracuse.

Yes, he went back to Syracuse that Friday, but not to Seymour Street. Wild, with no self-discipline, he went to see some of his buddies. After all, why spend time with us? That would be too important, and just as long as someone was watching Joanie and me, Pop had an excuse to go do his thing. He and his buddies spent the weekend drinking and playing cards. He didn't come home until Monday night. But he couldn't get into the house. The doors were locked.

Pop continued with his side of the story. Grandpa knew I was outside but he wouldn't let me in the house. After about ten minutes he finally came to the door, angrily speaking in Italian and broken English.

Where have you been?

Playing cards.

You been gambling all weekend?

Yes.

How much did you lose?

Weasel out of it with excuses, beat around the bush, become defensive, whichever one of these suited his need at that moment. That was Pop's style.

How much did you lose?

It's not like I lost it. I never really had it to begin with.

How much, Murph?

Three thousand.

You lost three thousand dollars!

Matto! Sei matto! You're crazy! He kept repeating over and over again. Times are bad. There's a war. There's rationing. Ma and I are watching your kids! You do remember the kids, don't you? And you're out running around with your buddies! Where do you get that kind of money to gamble with?

Playing cards at the base. That's how Joey wins his money.

How can you tell me you never had it to begin with?

Because I won it.

You also lost it! Couldn't you have saved it in the bank, like Joey does?

I have my whole life to save money. I needed this money now. I need to pay the bills.

You had the money! Then you lost the money! You could have paid all your bills with three thousand. Doesn't that tell you something, Murph? Why didn't you quit when you were ahead? Now as usual, you're broke!

I wanted more. I was having a good night and it would have helped out if I could have made more.

That's your problem. You don't know when to stop. You don't worry and you don't save money. And now you have been gone three days, gambling and drinking. You haven't spent any time with the twins. Jimmy's a devil. He's running all over like a wild animal. God forbid, he's going to be just like you. He has no discipline. He's going to be a problem. Joanie needs someone too. You lost all that money, and you haven't spent one day home since you came back from the base. If you ever do this again I will never let you in this house, and you will never see your kids again! Capisci!

Grandpa was right, Pop. How could you do that?

You need to understand what was happening at that time with mom, you and Joanie. It was tough for me being in the service.

That was Pop's M.O., vague and never to the point, beat around the bush. That's the way he operated.

The next day he went back to the base. Mom was getting worse and now Grandpa Corso was very ill. Grandma and the relatives couldn't keep taking care of us. Nobody could take care of us. Joanie and I were getting out of hand. Then suddenly, and I don't know how the arrangements were made, in December of 1944 Pop received an honorable discharge and came home permanently.

Magician's gig, the revolving door, he disappeared, then he was back. Mom disappeared, then she was back. Now we really didn't know who was in charge.

Pop's story continued. By the end of the year the TB sanitarium no longer could help your Mom. Her mental condition was really bad. And Grandpa Corso had what they called consumption. I think it was another name for cancer. I had to get permission to go back to Syracuse again, only this time under some bad circumstances.

As soon as I came home, I headed for Saranac Lake to see Dr. Trudeau.

He got right to the point. Lena is worse. Her TB is better, but emotionally she is terrible. I am going to recommend that you get her into the sanitarium in Syracuse. They have a good facility on Onondaga Hill. Are you familiar with the area?

Yeh, I know exactly where it is.

They can give her better treatment than we can here. We specialize in tuberculosis, not depression. I will make arrangements for you to check her in the hospital. Until then, she can go home and spend time with you and the twins. Maybe that will help with her depression. You should receive a phone call in a few days to check her into the hospital.

So Mom came home and I got an honorable discharge because of our family circumstances. Pop finished his wine, dropped his head to his chest and slowly started to drift into his afternoon nap. But he finished his story. In a few days, he said in a slow, sluggish voice, Mom was gone again and we were in a new year: 1945.

I don't know if it was sadness or pity, but my eyes were watering as I watched him drift off into his little nap. Maybe it was because he was so unhappy and lonely. He missed Mom. He was out of place here in Colorado. He belonged back in Syracuse, but he wouldn't go back. Everybody, friends and family, was gone. Colorado was supposed to be his future. But, for Pop, there was only the past. Pop never planned for the future, and sad to say, the future passed him by.

I picked up his glass, put it in the sink and placed his wine in the closet, and for some unspecific reason, I leaned over and kissed his little, bald head.

Chapter 7

I guess wine ran in our Italian veins. Grandpa Corso was an alcoholic. He could've had consumption or cancer too, but he definitely was an alcoholic. He loved his dago red wine and his Italian bread. He made all his own wine from his wine press in the cellar. And he took great pleasure in making his wine. He carried a jug of wine with him around the house, moving from room to room, eating a slice of bread and then washing it down with his homemade vino. Taking his shirtsleeve, he would wipe his mouth, then looking at me he would say, Buon gusto. Taste good. Jimmy boy, Buon gusto.

Grandpa became seriously ill. All those years of drinking finally caught up with him. At age 75 he was confined to bed for several weeks.

Vieni qua. Ho sete. Mi porti un bicchiere d'acqua, per favore, he would say. Please bring me a glass of water. I'm thirsty. Which Joanie and I did diligently every day he was in that bed.

Then one day Pop was looking out the front window when a square-backed truck pulled up in front of the house.

What's that, Dad?

That's the ambulance for Grandpa.

Why are they taking Grandpa?

He's very sick, Jimmy.

Two guys in white suits got out and went to the back of the truck, pulled out a bed and hurriedly came up to the front porch and into the house with Pop leading them to Grandpa's room.

A short time later they came out with Grandpa lying on this rolling bed, grandma walking beside him, holding his hand and crying.

Why is Grandma crying?

Because Grandpa is very sick.

Where're they taking Grandpa?

To the hospital.

I want to go with him.

No, you can't go.

Grandpa died at the hospital. Grandma cried, the Aunts cried, the Uncles were sad.

We buried grandpa in Assumption Cemetery.

Walking back to the car I saw a lady on her knees, screaming and crying and digging the dirt away from the grave, with two people trying to pull her away, but she angrily shoved them away and ran back to the grave, falling on her knees crying and again digging away the dirt.

How did Grandpa die?

He was sick.

What made him sick?

He was old with consumption.

What is that?

Something inside the body.

Will I die from that?

No, don't worry about it.

Will we ever see Grandpa again?

Someday, Jimmy. Hopefully, when we're all in heaven with God. We walked back to the car and headed to Seymour Street.

There were lots of people at the house gathered around tables filled with food. But everyone was silent. Uncle Gus stepped in front of one of the tables and gave a short talk. Then they all held up their wine glasses, and said, Salute to papa Corso who's now in heaven with our brother Larry. Grandma cried, the Aunts cried, the Uncles were sad.

Then grandma stepped forward and in her broken English thanked everyone for coming, and bringing all the food and said in Italian, Mangiamo, mangiamo. Let's eat, let's eat.

What's that, Pop?

Escargot. They're little snails. Just put them in butter and eat.

What's that one?

Calamari. It's like a fish with little legs. Try one. You'll like it. Try them I did, as I grabbed a toothpick and poked it into the little snail and swished it in the butter and slowly put it in my mouth. Then I did the same with the little fish with legs, feeling the crunching of the rubbery skin between my teeth.

What's that in your mouth, Jimmy?

A fish with legs.

Icky, how can you eat those things?

I like them. I shoved two more into my mouth.

Chapter 8

The weeks passed. The weather was nice, so Joanie and I could play outside. On one of those days, Pop yelled for us to come into the house. Running into the parlor we saw all the relatives gathered around the big floor standing radio, which stood about three feet high. They were listening to some man saying the war was over. Everyone was clapping, cheering, and all the Aunts were crying. I didn't understand how they could be happy and crying at the same time. Outside I heard the sounds of car horns blasting away in the street. Running to the window, I saw people jumping up and down, clapping, screaming, yelling, and hugging one another, and yes, the women were crying, but so were some of the men. I didn't understand what the war was, but whatever it was, it was finally over.

We know the war changed society. More and better products: from toothpaste to appliances to cars, and obviously, the television. It was a technological revolution, much like the technology of today. But for us it was the same old stuff. Mom was still in the sanitarium until the summer when she was allowed to spend some time at home. Even then things didn't seem to be getting any better for her. She especially wasn't coping with Grandma. I heard them one day having an argument in the kitchen.

You should have taken care of that a long time ago. You're not married in the eyes of God.

That's none of your business, Ma! That's between Jim and me!

It makes a difference to God!

And you shouldn't be snooping around in our room. What's in there is our business, not yours!

You haven't been around here, Lena. Augusto and I have been raising your kids, not you!

I can't help that I've been sick, and you know that!

Pop was in the parlor reading the paper. Walking over to him I asked him why Mom and grandma were arguing.

They just had a little disagreement, Jimmy. It's nothing serious.

But Mom is crying!

She's been sick. She's going through a tough time.

But why do they have to fight?

It's been hard for Grandma losing Grandpa, and she never recovered from Uncle Larry dieing. Don't worry. Things will get better.

But they didn't. She was angry and frustrated, unhappy and depressed, never understanding what was happening to her. But at least she was home that summer of '45, and Joanie and I were happy. At least until school started in the fall.

Jimmy, get up. It's time for school. You gotta go to school.

I don't want to go to school. Can't I stay home?

No. It's your first day. Joanie's already up and eating her breakfast. Besides, you'll like school. The nuns are nice. Now get dressed and I'll walk you and Joanie to school.

I'm four years, nine months old, entering my first day in Kindergarten, my first school, St. Lucy's.

Entering the building we went into a small hallway and down some stairs that led directly to the room. The nun greeted us at the door and told us to sit down in the chairs that were arranged in a circle. Joanie and I were frightened, but not crying like some of the other kids as their mothers kissed them good-by.

Talkative, brash and sassy, Joanie didn't frighten easily. Even in kindergarten she wasn't afraid to confront anyone, never hesitant to offer her opinion on anything. She definitely was the outgoing twin.

Joanie was also never afraid to stick up for me, challenging anyone who wanted to fight or hurt me. She even took on the kid next door who picked on me and pushed me around. The aggressive, classic bully. I was afraid to be near him, but not Joanie. After supper on that first day of school she saw him bullying me.

Get off of me, Halley. I whined.

Get off me, Halley! He mocked me to provoke me to fight back. Make me, Jimmy! Make me! How do you like eating dirt, Jimmy! Huh?

Get off my brother, Halley!

Yeh? Make me, Joanie!

I said, get off my brother! Now! She smacked him twice across the face. Now get off him!

She fought my battle for me in such an authoritative manner that it must have scared the crap out of Halley. All of a sudden he was off me, but not before he kicked more dirt in my face.

Gotta have your sister fight you battles for you, huh, Jimmy?

I didn't say anything, but he never bothered me again.

Watching from the porch were Pop and Uncle Joey. As I was brushing the dirt off I remember them congratulating Joanie for her fine job of handling Halley. Heck, I didn't care about pride. As long as he didn't bother me, and as long as I didn't have to fight him, I didn't care who beat him up, even if it was my sister.

Chapter 9

Mom left again and didn't come home until late spring 1946. For me, school was a disaster. I was glad the year was nearly over, weary of hearing the same litany from the ladies in the black and white habit.

Jimmy! Stay in your seat. You're not to get up and walk around the room!

Jimmy! Stay within the lines when you color.

Jimmy! Stay in your seat.

Jimmy! Help clean up on your table.

Jimmy! Stay in you seat.

Jimmy! Bless yourself when we say prayers!

Because Mom was home that spring, she took Joanie and me to school. On the last day of school Mom and I had a conference with Sister Claire.

Mrs. Corso, let me be very frank with you. Jimmy has no self-discipline. He doesn't stay in his seat. He too is too active a little boy. He lacks concentration and fails to follow instructions. Jimmy is not ready for first grade. I'm holding him back so he can repeat kindergarten. Mumbo jumbo. That's what the rest of the conversation was.

We left the building, Mom holding my hand. I was crying,

I don't want to repeat, Mom. I don't want to go back.

You have to. Sister Claire said you are not ready for first grade. You don't have enough self-control and you don't listen. You're behind the other kids, Jimmy. They're way ahead of you.

I don't like the nuns. They're mean and strict. You said the nuns would be nice.

They are nice, Jimmy.

No they're not! I want to stay with Joanie!

You can't stay with Joanie. That's it, Jimmy. No more questions. That's what happens when you don't do your schoolwork.

As the spring turned into summer, Mom was still home, but nobody knew for how long. We were together as a family, but it sure wasn't Ozzie and Harriet or Leave It to Beaver. Mom got upset very easily. And something was happening between her and Pop. Joanie and I started to see them, hear them, yelling and arguing.

You would think that after her problems with tuberculosis and being in the sanitarium they would get along together, more love and affection, but that would never, ever be the case in their marriage. Their arguing and fighting was a way of life for them, with Joanie and me loathing their fights. As the years went by, I would hate being near them or even in the house with them when they fought, longing to be old enough to escape so I wouldn't have to hear them.

And Mom's relationship with Grandma was getting worse. One hot, muggy, humid afternoon Mom and grandma had another big fight. Mom called a taxi then brought Joanie and me outside to the front porch to wait until the taxi arrived.

Where we going, Mom?

Aunt Connie's.

I need to go to the bathroom.

You should've gone before, Jimmy!

I didn't have to go before!

Slap! I felt the sting as her hand landed on my arm, which was becoming her favorite target. I'm angry and glaring at her, but too afraid to say anything.

You two, wait right here! Walking around to the back of the house, she got an empty milk bottle.

Here, hide behind the tree and go in the bottle!

Hide behind the tree Jimmy Boy did. Just enough so she couldn't see me. I was so angry that she made me do that, I took down my pants, and my underwear, daylight or not, and I didn't care who saw me, stark naked, peed in the bottle. I leaned back to make sure she wasn't watching me, so I could stay there a while longer, holding my manhood in my hand, well maybe not my manhood. At that age, I don't even think it was a boyhood.

Mom was changing. She reminded me of the nuns. No wonder she liked them.

Mom had set rules for dinner, for playing outside, for who we could and couldn't play with, and the most important rule of all, for Church. Ah, yes, Church. The most single, powerful force in our everyday lives. From morning when we opened our eyes, went to the bathroom, had breakfast, got dressed, played, went to school, came home, had supper and went to bed, it was the Church. Say your morning prayers, say your prayers at breakfast, say prayers at supper, say prayers at bedtime. It was the Church. It dominated our minds, our lives and, when we went to sleep, our dreams. As we got older, it was confession on Saturday, bless me Father for I have sinned. Penance. Church and communion on Sunday. Have a clean mind and soul. Have clean thoughts. Don't touch yourself. Mind the Ten Commandments. And the ultimate guilt trip of all: God will punish you! Sad to say, but it was the truth. The God I learned about in my early childhood and grew up with was a punishing, vindictive God.

But despite all her religious rituals, Mom was getting worse. Now it was Mom and Pop. Mom versus Pop.

Chapter 10

Pop liked to cook sometimes. One day he was making his homemade sauce in a large pot with one of his favorite meats, pig's feet. In a frying pan he sautéed garlic with olive oil and threw in some calamari. He would mix everything together, taste it by putting his finger in the pan, not enough salt, he would say, add more salt, taste it again, making sure it's right, then let it set overnight.

Lena, babe, homemade sauce is always best the next day, he would say.

That was a peaceful moment between them. But more and more I saw a side of them I had never seen before, the not so Christian side that would continue the rest of their lives. When we sat down for supper one day they were already very angry with each other, and Joanie and I were again wishing we could get out of the kitchen.

Jim, we've talked about this before. You're not paying the bills. She ate a piece of bread.

I pay the bills, Lena.

No you don't, Jim. That's why we get these phone calls about paying our bills.

Do you ever see our phone or lights turned off, Lena, or any of our furniture taken away?

This is what you always do! You turn things and twist them around as if everything is ok!

We always have food on the table. You've never seen us starve, have you? Pop's voice got louder with every response.

But we're behind on the light and phone bill, and we didn't make our last payment on the furniture!

I'll take care of that next month! I'll have some extra money!

Where are you going to get extra money?

I always win some playing cards with the guys.

You always lose! You don't think anything about gambling and drinking our money away, with nothing left for the bills!

Things always work out don't they, Lena? Then shoving a piece of meat in his mouth, he screamed, Ask God to pay the bills the next time you're on your knees!

I hope you choke on your food! She got up and angrily walked out of the kitchen, leaving Joanie and I to eat our supper in silence.

The next day they were at it again. I could see them yelling at each other as I approached the back porch, so I crept down to the cellar, my favorite escape, a good hiding place, plus I could play with Grandpa's wine press. Maybe that's why Grandpa drank so much wine. He needed to escape and what better place to do it than in the cellar making and drinking his wine. I missed Grandpa. I wished he were here so I could watch him make his wine.

I shut the cellar door because I didn't want to listen to them, but they were yelling so loud it didn't make any difference.

Damn you, Jim! I tired of this! We talked about this last night at supper!

God Damn you, Lena. Why don't you be more cooperative?

Don't take the Lord's name in vain! I am being cooperative! We need to pay our bills!

Lena, you worry too damn much. Everything will work out! You don't ever see me worrying!

That's exactly your problem, Jim. You don't care! You don't worry!

You need to pray more, Lena. Maybe then God will help you pay the bills!

That made her furious and she threw a pot at Pop.

Now why did you do that? And then he laughed.

That must have made her even more angry because she threw another pot at Pop. Then I heard crash, crash, and crash! After a few moments there was complete silence. I slinked up the cellar stairs and peeked in the kitchen. They were gone but there were pots and pans all over the floor. With a nervous, sick feeling in my stomach, I went back down the cellar to hide.

All this fighting caused Joanie and I also to fight.

Maybe that's why I thought fighting was just a way of life for a man and a woman.

Maybe that's why it took me many years to realize that this wasn't the way to treat women. They wanted to be treated with understanding, tenderness, respect and love. Pop never learned that.

Chapter 11

Several weeks later Mom talked to me about enrolling in a new school for that fall.

Jimmy, how would you like to go to St. Joseph's?

Why, what's wrong with St. Lucy's?

We think it's best if you try a new school. Things might be better for you for learning and doing your schoolwork.

No, I don't want to go. I want to stay at St. Lucy's so I can be near Joanie.

You're going to have to go to St. Joseph's whether you like it or not. That's it. We think you'll do better there than at St. Lucy's. Besides the nuns are nicer than at St. Lucy's.

But something must have happened because three months later I was back in Kindergarten at St. Lucy's, confusing me more than ever. Maybe the nuns at St. Joseph's couldn't handle me or maybe I still wasn't getting my work done. Whatever the cause, whatever the reason, by the start of January, I was back in familiar territory.

Kindergarten is wonderful the second time around. Not exactly, but in the spring of '47, I finally, barely, passed kindergarten. The nuns still weren't happy with my work so they must have given me what was called a social pass, just glad to get rid of me.

Mrs. Corso, we're going to pass Jimmy. We can't keep him another year in kindergarten. He's going to be too old, and the other kids will make fun of him. Jimmy needs lots of help. He's very slow, and is still behind the other kids. He should be in first grade and he barely can do his kindergarten schoolwork. He still has no self-discipline, and he doesn't follow directions. He should be starting to read and pronounce easy words. You're really going to have to work with him or he won't do well next year in first grade. Then he'll be even further behind kids his own age.

But home wasn't a helpful place. The fighting between Mom and Pop was getting even worse, if that was possible. As the year progressed I learned another way, other than hiding in the cellar, to escape the constant fighting and my discontent about going to school. Music.

One night, not answering Mom, knowing it was bedtime but hoping to be so quiet she would think I had gone to bed, I turned off the parlor lights and sat down next to the our big old radio, listening and gently rocking back and forth to the music. But hearing the radio, she came into the room and turned on the lights.

What are you doing, Jimmy?

Nothing. I'm just listening to the music.

It's time for bed.

Can I stay just stay a few more minutes?

She stood there a while, pondering what to say, and finally said OK, a few more minutes, then go to bed.

I went back to my rocking. Wow! It felt good. I guess it soothed my insecurity, and the more I did it, the more I liked it. I became a rocker.

I would rock in the chair, on the floor, in the bed. One night I made so much noise that Mom and Pop discovered my little dirty secret.

What are you doing?

Nothing.

Is that noise we heard you rocking the bed?

Yeh, I guess.

Well, knock it off and go to sleep!

Okay.

Of course I didn't listen to them. I wasn't going to give up something that made me feel good and was a great way to release pent up energy. I just toned down my rocking to a quieter level, rock, rock, rock.

I continued this bad, or maybe a good, habit of rocking into my early teen years, compensating for the stress of my life by rocking. Rocking.

To this day I still love rocking, only I rock in my ancient, big, tan rocking chair held together with duct tape. Karren hates the chair, always asking me what are the chances I will get rid of it. Slim and none. Slim and none. Slim and none.

I keep everything, get rid of nothing, your connoisseur, all American pack rat. Because something is old, doesn't mean it needs to be thrown away. I lost so many childhood mementos because we moved so often that I now over-compensate by saving things, regardless of their value.

———————————————

Chapter 12

Hating the nuns. Hating school. Six years old in the fall of 1947, I grudgingly entered first grade at St. Lucy's. The nuns ruled with fear and terror.

Heads rolled on Mondays, when the black and white homeroom sisters, with never a smile on their faces, demanded, Who didn't go to church yesterday?

Those of us who raised our hands were sent to Mother Superior's office to face her wrath. She wanted to teach us bad children a lesson about not attending church. After all, we probably were expected to get our parents out of bed on Sunday morning and take them to church. Fat chance of us telling our parents what to do when many of them had been though two wars, food rationing and a depression.

Entering the main office, I saw Joanie, so we stood together in line waiting for our turn to explain why we didn't attend church yesterday. God forbid the nuns should go to the parents and ask them. We faced Mother Superior, a small, puffy-cheeked, heavy-set woman wearing glasses. Arrogant and pompous, she feared no one. I looked back behind me and saw a long line of kids that extended out of the office and down the hallway. Judging by the line, I would say yesterday was a slow day for God.

Peering over her glasses and in a very stern voice she exhorted, Come forward you two and tell me your names!

Fearing her and shy, I kept silent, my head down, looking at my shoes, and let Joanie do the talking.

Joanie and Jimmy Corso! Joanie said sarcastically and defiantly.

Did you go to church on Sunday?

No, said Joanie, with a snarl on her face and a growl in her voice, shaking her head back and forth, again defiantly.

Why? She was writing something in her "log book". Maybe she was keeping track so God could see it when we died.

How do we know? sneered Joanie. Why don't you ask our parents?

Mother Superior angrily peered over her glasses.

You better watch your tongue, young lady, or you'll being staying after school learning to show respect.

Of course, the congregation of parents knew this little game was happening every Monday, but no one ever dared to say anything to the nuns or priests. It was a sign of the times. The parents did what they were supposed to do, kept their mouths shut. Don't question anything. "Do as I say not as I do."

I often wondered how many years the school played this little charade of terror, frightening the children as if it was their fault they didn't go to church on Sundays.

The next day being in a rare, happy mood, whistling and ready to hang up my jacket in the coatroom, I was shoved hard from behind and was nose to nose with an angry nun. She grabbed me and shook the daylights out of me, pinning me against the rack, yelling in my face. I peed my pants.

Don't you ever come into this school whistling again! Do you understand me? This is not your home. This is a place of God!

Spit in her face, scream at her, or just rip her arms off her body. These were my impulsive instincts, but frozen scared and on the verge of crying, silence was always the best approach.

Yes sister, I'll never do it again. What kind of a nun was this? Maybe I should have come into the coatroom saying shit, or Goddamn, giving her a real reason to go into her tirade.

That night at supper Joanie was talking about the cheerleaders at school.

I want to be a cheerleader. When can I try out?

You'll need to ask the nuns, said Mom.

What do I have.

Interrupting her I blurted out what happened at school. After a few moments of silence, Mom responded, Well, Jimmy, you shouldn't have been whistling in school.

What's wrong with whistling? And she didn't have to shove me against the coat rack!

She did it because you deserved it.

Why is it so bad? Is God angry with me? Am I going to hell for whistling?

Of course not, but the nuns need to keep the school quiet or the kids will always be raising hell. That was Pop's answer to my problem.

I was about to say something, but I knew it wouldn't do any good to complain. The nuns ruled, and Mom and Pop were not interested in our problems at school. Again silence was the best policy.

After supper I went into the parlor and listened to the radio. Some guy named Bing Crosby was singing, but I wasn't interested in him, so I changed the station and listened to one of the big bands. It might have been Benny Goodman or Glen Miller or Duke Ellington or Count Basie. I don't remember which one. I could never keep them straight. I just sat down next to the radio and did what was made me feel good. Rocking. Back and forth. Back and forth.

Chapter 13

Somehow I managed to get through the first grade. I'm not sure how because the nuns were not satisfied with my progress.

At home Mom wasn't getting any better, showing increasing signs of frustration and memory lapses, and growing really tired of living with so many people. She wanted out, but there was no place to go, no place to live because Pop was content staying at Seymour Street. He had left the steel mill and taken a job at the bakery just down the street, requiring him to be at work at five in the morning. Seymour Street was convenient for Pop so we stayed.

We never did much as a family. There were no vacations. Pop went to work, and Mom, like most mothers of that era, stayed home with the kids. However, on rare occasions, the four of us would go downtown to the stores. As we were walking past a furniture store we saw a strange box with people in it.

What's that, dad? asked Joanie.

It's called a television.

What does it do?

Pop gave a brief explanation, but we didn't understand what he was talking about. I didn't dare ask how those people could get into such a small box.

Can we afford one?

Someday soon, he said, not looking at Mom.

Food and gas were the only priorities on his list. He paid in cash, grudgingly. And on any item he was able to charge, clothing or furniture or whatever, he was always late paying the bill, or would even miss a payment telling them he would pay double next time, which he never did. This worked for a while, but the businesses were on to his scheme. His real money went to alcohol and playing cards with the guys or for whatever he wanted to do and the hell with the bills. It would be only a matter of time before the bill collectors came knocking at the door.

In the meantime there was, as Pop always said, food on the table.

Arriving home for supper through the back door, I could smell the sweet aroma of hot, homemade Italian bread. Grandma was standing over the oven holding a large can of olive oil, pouring it over a split loaf of bread she then sprinkled Parmesan cheese over. In a big pot on the stove was hot homemade minestrone soup and a pot each of calamari and escargot. Grandma turned around, never making eye contact with Mom. Mom avoided her by going around the other end of the table.

Sederti, sit down, supper is ready, Mangia. Maybe it was her way of saying she was sorry for all of us sitting down to another angry, but quiet, supper.

Mangia I did, scarfing down the homemade soup, followed by mouthfuls of calamari, escargot and hot bread and butter.

Slow down, Jimmy, you're eating too fast. Don't stuff your mouth.

This is how I always eat, Mom, you know that. My usual sarcastic response, while I continued to swallow my food as fast as I could get it into my mouth.

And eat everything on your plate. Don't waste any food. There are boys and girls in world who are starving because they don't have anything to eat. It's a sin to throw away food. Eat. It's God will.

Chapter 14

The good news was that in the fall of 1948, I entered second grade at St. Lucy's. The bad news is Mom and Pop should have been happy for me, but it didn't matter to them that I made it to second grade in one try. Mom was often angry and fighting with Pop who was his usual aloof self, letting the bills slide for another month, causing more arguments. No end in sight.

And why should their attitude be any different? Either they didn't want to change, didn't know how to change, or they just didn't give a damn about their constant quarreling or how it would affect Joanie and me.

One time, however, much to my bewilderment, we actually experienced a very pleasant moment, at least in appearance. Sometimes Mom, Pop, Shirley, Donnie, and whoever else was around, would pull back the rug in the parlor and dance.

Let's cut a rug! yelled Shirley. Turn up the radio!

I'll do that! yelled Donnie in delight. They were the cousins that loved to have fun, laugh and dance to something called the Jitterbug.

Mom and Pop held hands and then would dance to the slower music especially if they heard the "Wedding Anniversary" song, supposedly their favorite song. Now, if that didn't beat all. Someone needed to enlighten me as to how they could fight constantly, practically ruin their marriage, make their kids paranoid and insecure, and then once in a blue moon, dance and hold hands as if everything was peachy and warm, then fight and yell at each other tomorrow, the next day, the next week, the next month, the next year.

Pop was an amateur ballroom dancer before he met Mom. He and his partner won several trophies in competition, but true to his character and style, he didn't care about saving mementos and instead gave them to his partner.

But he wasn't only good at shuffling his feet, he also played the piano, by ear. Never wanting nor having the patience to read sheet music, he had the rare and uncanny ability to listen to a song and then play the music.

Why do I need to read all those notes? I've got my ears and I can hear and play the music. It's faster and easier. That summed up his attitude: faster and easier, the "band-aid" philosophy, fix it temporarily and it solves all the problems. No patience to follow up on his work.

He wasted so much of his talent. Pop was not only one heck of a football player in high school, but he also could handle a glove and bat so well that he actually played semi-pro baseball.

Why didn't you stick it out and try pro ball, Pop?

Why should I? I'd have to go to practice every day and work extra hard on special plays and batting and all that stuff. Too many small details that coaches have you go over and over again. I don't have time for any of that small detail stuff. I have other things to do.

Chapter 15

Second grade was another difficult year for me. Another year lacking arithmetic skills, reading skills, not to mention social skills. Another year of falling farther behind the other kids. I was really looking forward to it. Failing that is.

Just before Christmas vacation the nuns requested a talk with Mom and Pop, and, of course, me. It seemed like an eternity sitting outside the office waiting for Mother Superior to talk to us. Finally she opened the door and asked us to come in. Sitting down and peering over her glasses, she got right to the point, but what the heck, we knew each other already. After all, I had been in her office all those Monday mornings when we didn't go to church, and she knew my transcript like the back of her hand. Keep in mind I had failed kindergarten and almost flunked first grade. While she had Mom and Pop in here why didn't she ask them about not going to church on Sundays? Was she a scaredy-cat? I was chuckling to myself, but I was definitely keeping my head down so they couldn't see me.

Let me get directly to the point, Mr. and Mrs. Corso. Jimmy's not doing well in his classes. With my head down, I was mocking her under my breath. I had her almost word for word. Jimmy's not doing well in his classes. He repeated kindergarten, barely got by first grade, and now he is struggling in second grade. His reading and math skills are on a kindergarten level, and he is falling way behind the other kids.

It was the same mumbo jumbo all over again.

We realize he is slow, Mother Superior. Jimmy has always been a slow leaner and has a difficult time remembering, but his skills can't be that bad.

Yes, they are, Mrs. Corso. You may not be aware of it, but Jimmy has some very severe learning problems! We're going to have to correct them now or it will be impossible for him to make it though elementary school let alone high school.

But he passed first grade.

Yes, Mrs. Corso, thanks to Sister Mary. She couldn't hold him back another year or the kids would have made fun of him. After that comment Mom and Pop didn't say anything, probably because they didn't know what to say.

So what can we do? Pop finally said, trying to impress her that he really cared.

He needs special attention with lots of individual help! You might try reading to him and having him read to you, making sure he sounds out the words slowly and carefully. Work on the vowels, a, e, i, o, u. You do remember your vowels, don't you?

Mom was smiling, but she was probably also remembering she was a sixth grade drop out.

Help him with his numbers. Do it on paper, use your hands, toothpicks, silverware, anything that will help him understand adding and subtracting. The more you work with him, the better he will get. If not, it will be another year of falling behind.

With that all said, I was feeling like Dopey, but her assessment was accurate. If I didn't get it now, it would be too late.

Okay, then if you don't have any questions, I would recommend that we meet again sometime in the next few months to discuss his progress.

It was the same old thing. Mom talked. Pop talked. Mother superior talked. As always, I never said anything, silent, my head down, looking at the floor and shuffling my feet back and forth, not caring what they said.

But I did care that they never asked me what I thought my problem was. They never asked my feelings or what I thought I could do to help myself. Not caring at all what I thought, just a little boy who didn't count! If I counted, if the nuns, Mom or Pop really cared, they would have worked with me, helped me after school, got me a tutor and spent time with me. That never happened. Nobody ever helped me with my numbers. Nobody ever read to me or helped me with my vowels. I drifted in my own little dream world, not caring about arithmetic, reading or school. I didn't fall through the cracks in the system. I wasn't even really in the system.

I failed second grade. The nuns gave up on me. Mom gave up on me. Pop gave up on me. I gave up on me. No confidence in myself and what I was doing. My self-image, my self-worth, my pride was down the toilet. Angry at the church, the priests, the nuns, and myself. Wondering, cynically, is this God's will?

Chapter 16

The meeting that was supposed to occur later in the school year did not happen nor would it have made any difference. Mom had a complete breakdown and Pop decided a change might do her some good.

What's the matter? I asked, startled to see Mom crying and sitting on Pop's lap.

We're just talking. Where's Joanie?

She's outside. She's coming back from the park with Uncle. . .

Tell her to come in. I want to talk to both of you.

Joanie was getting out of the car, but she sure looked squirmy and uneasy, her eyes glazed. Fidgety and nervous.

What's the matter, Joanie?

Nothing! she said sarcastically. Why?

You've been crying?

No! It's none of your business! Leave me alone!

Dad wants to talk to us.

Entering the parlor, Pop looked at Joanie intensely. Why is your face so red?

I've just been running in the park that's all. What do you want?

How would you like to move?

Why? Joanie asked with a sarcastic smirk on her face.

Because. We need to.

I guess, said Joanie. Where're we going?

We are moving in with Grandma and Grandpa Colella.

My eyes bulged out of my eye sockets, and I cried out, I don't want to go! I don't like that old, cold, damn house! You would have thought I'd taken the Lord's name in vain. Mom, jumped off of Pop's lap, red eyes

55

and all, came right at me, slapping me on the arms and yelling,You stop talking like that!

I wanted to say Damn! Damn! Goddamn! With my smart-ass mouth, but knowing how Mom would react, I nonchalantly said, Dad and the Uncles talk like that all the time.

Never mind dad and the Uncles! You're not to say that word or I'll wash your mouth out with soap! It's God's will for us to go there!

Of course, I thought to myself, how stupid of me for not knowing that it was God's will for us to be going there.

But I don't want to go. I don't like that old, stinky, broken down house. Making sure I didn't use the. . uh… damn word.

Stop talking like that! God will punish you for acting like that. We're lucky we have a place to live.

Ah, yes, now it's the "God will punish you" lecture. Something new. Between God's will and God's punishment, I wonder if I'll ever make it to heaven?

There was no sense in arguing. September of 1949 we went to live with Grandma and Grandpa Colella.

Emotionally weak, in a fragile state of mind, Mom was gradually slipping into despair and another bout with depression. But for me it was the house.

I didn't want to live there on "shanty hill". It was a very old house. Rickety and beyond repair, and lop-sided because it was built on a slope and located in the middle of about fifteen houses on a old, bumpy dirt road, so narrow it was impossible for two cars to go by each other at the same time. Twenty yards from the railroad tracks and the trains that rattled the house every time they went by.

Pop parked his car on the road next to the house. On snowy and rainy days the car was a mess from being splashed by passing cars. Pop hated cleaning those windows.

The front steps to the house were weak and creaky. The porch door was barely hanging by its hinges. The dirt-covered windows were not sealed, letting in the cold winter winds that chilled our bodies to the bones.

Against the windows, was a square white box that had ice blocks in it to keep the food cold. In the front window Mom would have to put a white card with black numbers 10, 15, 25, indicating the pounds we needed for the day. Even back on Seymour Street we had already gone from an ice-a-box to a modern refrigerator.

Opening the door to the kitchen I was stunned by the foul smell. It came from the empty and half-filled wine and beer bottles that were spewed on the sticky, dirty floors.

In the center of the room was an old table surrounded by four chairs. Hanging from the ceiling over the table was a cord that had a single light bulb attached to it, the only source of light for the kitchen. Against the wall was an old gas stove. Next to it was an old fashioned, one piece, freestanding sink that was filled with dirty dishes. Walking from the kitchen I went into the dining room that had one large floor grate that served as the only source of heat for the first floor. Next to the dining room was a bedroom where Uncle Billy and Uncle Victor slept. Peeking into the room I could see filthy sheets on the unmade beds and clothes and beer bottles scattered all over the room. To my right was the parlor. Located next to the wall I could hardly believe what I saw. It was one of those square boxes that showed little people inside it. A television set. Passing the windows I brushed against the light-brown curtains causing a puff of dust. Around the corner I went up the creaky stairs that lead directly to the bathroom that the eight of us had to share. In front of the bathroom was a small floor grate that was the only source of heat for the upstairs.

Walking back to the kitchen I passed the stairs that led to the cellar. There a coal burning stove provided heat for the house, but never enough to keep out the cold, harsh bitter New York winds. I walked through the kitchen to the back porch where grandma and grandpa slept.

As I stepped down into the back yard, I was under a covering of grapevines attached to a network of wood structures. These were nailed to the roof and strung along the side and back of the house. This tiny island of calm provided a place for me to hide or to escape the turmoil of the house.

Straight ahead I climbed a set of stairs that led to a row of old, dirty, empty chicken coops covered with pigeon poop which now served only as a shelter for mice. Somehow the mice always found their way into the kitchen, scurrying around the sink and pantry for bits of food.

This was the squalor and decay of Kingsley Place and the Colellas versus the cleanliness of Seymour Street and the Corsos who at least were trying to join middle class and make real their American dream.

This is a dump, I mumbled to myself, making sure I didn't say it loud enough in front of Mom or it would have been God's will to punish me. I guess I was becoming cynical not only about the Church but about my life in general. When I walked back into the house I asked Pop why we were moving.

I sold the house to Uncle Joey.

I didn't know what to say. I just looked at him in disgust.

I work hard all day. When I come home I don't want to be bothered with repairs to the house. I want to sit and relax. Part of the deal was he had to take grandma with him when he sells the house. They get along great.

He was lying. It was the same old story. Pop had avoided paying his bills. He literally ran away from his problems thinking things would get better. That the grass would be greener. But things never got better, only worse. The grass was always browner.

The truth about moving probably had to do with Mom's relationship with Grandma. It had decayed to such a condition that they no longer even talked to each other. Mom wanted out of what she considered a living nightmare. But in a way she was in her own nightmare. Living with the "demons" inside her that she couldn't control.

Much later in my life, to put things in perspective about Grandma Corso, I called my cousin Donnie to see if he could give me any information he could about her.

Grandma Corso was the devil incarnate, Jimmy.

The devil incarnate?

Yeh. She always argued with my mother.

I always thought only my Mom and Grandma fought.

Grandma had differences with a lot of the family. In fact, one day I became suspicious about her activities. When I came home from school my parents were out for the day. When I opened the front door to go upstairs I saw grandma coming out of our apartment. I quickly went back outside so she wouldn't see me.

I wouldn't have given it any thought except it happened several more times. One time, curious about why she was doing this, I told her that I was going out to play. Instead I snuck back into our apartment and hid under my parents' bed. After a short time I heard her quietly coming into the room. She proceeded to open a number of drawers and look under the clothes, making sure she put them back in proper order. Standing there for a short time, she tapped her fingers on the dresser. She then went to the closet. Not finding anything, she left.

I told my mother what happened. She didn't say anything except, thank you. I don't think she told anyone, including my dad.

The devil incarnate was quiet a revelation to me. The dark and shady side of Grandma Corso I never knew. There was more happening in the house than anyone realized.

In the fall of 1949 I enrolled in Porter. My fourth school in four years. Just another long school year for me. Emotionally I couldn't understand why I was still struggling repeating second grade. Whatever the reason, I was now sure of the fact that I would never succeed in school. I was a failure and I would always be a failure.

Living with Grandpa and my Uncles at the Colellas was a terrible experience. It was a nightmare. What stunned me the most was the relationship between them. How they treated each other was shocking.

Pop once told me that Uncle Billy served on the front lines on D-day. Whether that was true or not, it still shouldn't have been an excuse to be constantly drunk and not hold a steady job.

Uncle Victor was also a total waste. He never worked and was always in and out of detoxification. He didn't care, or maybe he did, but couldn't do anything about it.

And Grandpa had no clue how to be a father. Always drinking. Every day.

The weekends were the worst. One Sunday night I was lying in bed, dreading school the next day. I finally dozed off to sleep only to be awakened by two voices screaming at each other. Jumping out of bed, I hurried downstairs and into the kitchen. The voices belonged Uncle Billy and Grandpa. They were ready to kill each other. Grandpa was yelling at Uncle Billy in broken English.

Why you no get job and go to work?

I have a job!

Suddenly it got violent. Uncle Billy shoved grandpa so hard that his head snapped against the wall. Grandpa retaliated by hitting Uncle Billy, grazing his cheek, and causing a trickle of blood from his mouth.

You have no steady job! You stay short time then quit! No work! Sit around house all day! You no work since you home from war!

What would you know! You were never in the war! You don't know what it's like seeing your buddies die in front of you!

No excusa! You get job! Get married! Have family!

That's none of your business!

You like Victor. No steady work. No money! Always ask money for drink!

What about you?! Always drinking! Always drunk!

Grandpa angrily said something in Italian that I didn't understand. Then he shouted, I work for money! No ask or take from anyone!

Then the unthinkable happened. Uncle Billy doubled up his right fist and swung at Grandpa, grazing the right side of his head. I stepped between them, trying to separate them, crying for them to stop. But Uncle Billy just pushed me aside, laughing, then went back after Grandpa.

Realizing I couldn't do anything I went back upstairs. I couldn't believe it. It was like a street fight. Between a father and a son. Hitting each other as if they were mortal enemies.

Disagreements on the Corso side were common and sometimes very heated. But they never hit each other. Walking back to bed I had a sick feeling, a big knot in my stomach. Scared, but knowing there was nothing I could do to stop them. I rocked myself to sleep.

The next morning at breakfast I wanted to say something to Mom but didn't know how to say it. In fact she was humming and in a good mood today. So different from those other times when she was sad. It was if she had two different personalities. One time she'd be happy. Then she'd be sad. Outgoing, then secluded, as if she'd lost touch with her surroundings. She sure acted weird.

What do you want for breakfast, Jimmy?

I don't care. Not making eye contact with her.

What's wrong, Jimmy?

Nothing.

Yes, there is.

I told you, nothing!

Well, whatever the reason, hurry and eat your breakfast. You're gonna be late for school.

I don't care if I'm late. I hate school! I don't like the teachers or the kids. Who cares if I'm not there.

Stop talking like that. Now finish your breakfast and go to school.

On my way to school I kept thinking how to tell her or even if I should tell her. Maybe it would be best if I didn't say anything. It bothered me all day, not telling her about the fight.

After school Mom was ironing clothes in the dining room. She was sprinkling Pop's shirts with one of those soda bottles filled with water and a cork top with holes. Much to my surprise, I blurted out, Mom, Grandpa and Uncle Billy had a big fight last night!

Well, they disagree sometimes. Just like the Corsos.

They had a bad fight.

Jimmy, ever since the end of the war Uncle Billy and Uncle Victor have changed. They started to drink. And.

They hit each other, Mom!

That must have gotten her attention because she stopped ironing.

What do you mean they hit each other?

They grabbed and hit each other. I tried to stop them but Uncle Billy just pushed me away. He just laughed at me.

I'll say something to them tonight. Now go outside and play.

Later, walking into the kitchen for supper, I saw Grandpa and Uncle Billy sitting opposite each other at the table.

Slouching over to the table, I reluctantly sat down in the empty chair between them. Grandpa took a swallow of wine, leaving a dribble on his mustache, that then dripped down the stubble of his black and white beard and onto the raggedy old sport coat he always wore. His cold blue eyes were hard and distant. He looked only at Tippy our dog, and never acknowledged me. Wiping spaghetti from his mustache, he leaned over and gave Tippy a plate of spaghetti and meatballs. Mangia! he laughed.

How ya doing kid? said Uncle Billy as he peered over his glasses and took a swallow of wine.

I mumbled, okay, giving him a quick stare.

Mom gave me a plate of spaghetti and pig's feet. After a few bites I was chuckling to myself.

What's so funny Jimmy?

I saw this funny looking drawing on the chicken coop when I was playing hide-and-seek. It was a face with two eyes and a big nose. It looked like the guy's hands were over a fence or something, and it said, Kilroy was here.

That was started overseas, said Uncle Billy. It was everywhere.

What does it mean? Still not looking at him.

I don't know what it means, but many of our boys would make the drawing in bars, buildings, bathrooms and just about anywhere. Then they brought it over here.

After supper Joanie and I went into the parlor and turned on the T.V. We had three stations to choose from which we thought was great. As the T.V. slowly warmed up we saw a bunch of kids about five years old sitting in some stands called the Peanut Gallery. Standing in front of the gallery was a clown and a guy named Buffalo Bob asking the kids, What time is it? It's Howdy Doody Time!

That T.V set with the people inside it would dominate our lives. It was our salvation and put us into another world, a temporary escape from our every day problems.

But we couldn't really escape, and the problems kept getting worse. Saturday morning we were playing down the street with some kids when one of the girls got mad and shoved Joanie. She retaliated by hitting the girl and was ready to hit her brother, Frankie. Immediately I ran over and defended Joanie by punching Frankie. But it didn't faze him. Within seconds he was on top of me squeezing my head so hard that it was ringing like a bell. God, I wished I was Rocky Graziano. I could hear Joanie yelling, Get him Jimmy. But I wasn't getting him. Somehow I needed to get out of this fight. So I did what any brave young man would do when losing a fight. I bit him. He immediately released me, crying and yelling, He bit me! His mom came running out of the house to see what the commotion was about, but I wasn't about to stay. I was running down the dirt road heading for the quiet of the grapevines. I sat there a long time next to Tippy.

I was there until I heard Mom calling me out the back door. Walking into the kitchen I saw Frankie and his mother talking to Mom and Joanie.

Look at his arm! she yelled.

Boys will be boys, said Mom.

He left teeth marks on Frankie's arm! What kind of boy are you raising?

I'm raising a good boy. Jimmy will be punished for doing this.

I hope so! If you don't punish that boy he'll wind up in jail! She slammed the door behind her as they left.

Joanie and I explained who started the fight.

I don't care if they started it or not! No more fights! And don't bite anyone again! You and Joanie are not to go over there again! Stay away from those kids! I don't want any more trouble! I have enough of my own!

That night Mom and Pop went out for the evening. On their way out they yelled that Uncle Billy was going to watch us for the night.

Why Uncle Billy! Can't we have Aunt Angie or cousin Vickie?

No. Uncle Billy will be just fine. There won't be any problems.

He can't even take care of himself. How's he going to take care of us?

He'll be just fine, Joanie. We bought soda and chips for you. After "Your Show of Shows" you get to bed.

Lying in bed, I was enjoying the unusual quietness of the house, and I went to sleep but I was awakened again by the yelling. What's Uncle Billy doing now? I got out of bed and went down to the kitchen. But it wasn't Uncle Billy. It was Uncle Victor and Grandpa arguing with each other. I couldn't believe it. Their arguing turned into grabbing and shoving each other with the same violence as Uncle Billy and Grandpa. I thought about trying to separate them, but knowing I couldn't do anything, I just went upstairs to bed and rocked myself to sleep.

The next day Mom was sweeping the kitchen floor. I told her what happened but she gave me the same answer. I'll talk to them, later. Then she went back to sweeping the floor.

But she never said anything to them. She didn't care. They didn't care. I didn't care.

Staying out of trouble wasn't getting any easier for me. A few days later I got in a fight with Gary who lived directly across the tracks from us. We were rolling on the ground. The kids were yelling so loud that I could barely hear Pop calling me. When I got up to leave I was yelling and screaming at Gary. My shirt was torn and I had a hole in my trousers. When Mom sees me I'm in real trouble.

Jimmy! Get in here now! came the booming voice.

You better go, you big sissy! Go home to your mommy and daddy, you chicken!

That made me furious. Even knowing that most guys could beat me up, I still never backed down from anyone. Crying and mad, I picked up a rock and threw it at him. Luckily, I missed him. But the rock shattered the parlor window of his house. Realizing what I did, I ran home. Sprinting up the little hill and up the front steps, I passed Tippy and the cat and ran straight into Pop's triple E foot. That made me cry harder.

When I call you to come home I mean now, not tomorrow!

In the kitchen Mom was on the phone talking to Gary's mom. Hanging up the phone, she went into her lecture about responsibility and fighting.

What's wrong with you! This is the second fight since we've been here! And what did I always tell you about throwing things? You could have really hurt him.

Leave him alone, Lena. He has to learn to fight his own battles. You can't baby the boy his whole life.

You're mad at him too!

I'm mad because he didn't come when I called him. Not because he was in a fight. He has to learn to be a man. To stand up to people and not have them push him around.

Me getting into fights was nothing compared to Joanie's mysterious and unexplained actions.

One afternoon I headed to the bathroom. Lifting the seat I saw a humongous spider. Just as I was ready to flush it down the toilet I heard Mom and Joanie whispering underneath the upstairs heat grate. Curious as to why they were so quiet, I didn't flush the toilet so they wouldn't know I was upstairs. I quietly walked over to the grate and knelt down to listen. Joanie was crying and I could barely hear what she was saying about some Uncle.

He took his hand…put …,her voice fading off then rising again. Then he un… her voice faded again.

What did he do next? whispered Mom.

I couldn't hear what they said next, except when Mom asked how long it had been going on.

Since I was seven

Where has this been happening?

At the park, when we were in the car. In the parlor, when everybody else was in the kitchen.

Suddenly grandpa's voice called out for Mom and they both stopped talking. I couldn't put the puzzle together. I didn't know what was happening or who they were talking about.

Everything was quiet for the next week until Mom and Pop went out that Saturday night. They trusted that everything would be okay so we stayed by ourselves. After watching T.V. Joanie and I went to bed.

But I didn't sleep. My stomach was churning. I knew the inevitable was going to happen. And it did. This time it was the three of them. All drunk. Uncle Billy swaying back and forth. Uncle Victor a mess. His shirt outside of his unzipped trousers. Grandpa stared stony eyed at both of them. They could almost have been the Three Stooges, except it wasn't funny. All three yelling at each other in Italian. What a waste of human life.

Uncle Victor and Uncle Billy grabbed and punched each other. I tried separating them, but they just pushed me aside. Grandpa said something to them in Italian. He was angry at both of them and ready to fight them both.

I screamed. Stop it! What's the matter with you! You are crazy! Maybe you should just kill each other so we can have some peace and quiet!

I must have accomplished something because they immediately stopped. They looked at each other, knowing that this time they had gone too far. I went back upstairs and didn't care if they hurt each other. It was too much. Constantly getting drunk then fighting. They acted like animals in a zoo. I didn't need to visit a zoo. I was living in one. Rock, rock.

The next day, again, I said something to Mom. Again, she said she would talk to them later. But it was always later. Nothing ever was said, or if she did say something it didn't do any good. I went outside under the grapevines and sat down next to Tippy. I kept wishing we were back at Seymour Street. There the rooms were clean and every room had heat. They had their disagreements, but they never came home drunk and hit each other.

Chapter 17

The year passed from Christmas to the New Year, 1950, and the start of second semester. Again, I hadn't accomplished anything in school. I didn't pass math or English. My writing was very poor.

When I walked into the classroom I took the same seat as last semester. All the kids except me were talking and catching up with each other as if they hadn't seen one another in years. The teacher was standing in front of the classroom trying to get our attention.

People, would you please sit down and be quiet. Good morning, and welcome back for the new semester. I hope, blah, blah, blah. I tuned her out. Didn't want to listen. Who cares? Blah, Blah, Blah.

Before we start our new material we are going to make some changes. The following students will be going next door for some special help.

Special help? Schoolwork? She had my attention. I wonder what she meant? It didn't sound good.

Special help? I wonder if I am in that group? She read the names of several students, eventually calling my name.

Special help? Why did she say that in front of all the kids? Good students don't need special help. But us dummies, we do. She might as well have announced it to the whole school.

Just like before Christmas when she gave us a big test worth 100 points, then read the scores in front of the class. All the kids knew I got the lowest score in the class, a 27.

I looked down at the floor, hoping the kids would ignore me, pretending that I really didn't care. But it was embarrassing to be singled out in front of the whole class.

I got up with the other students and slouched into the next room where a lady teacher was waiting for us.

Please be seated. You're probably wondering why we separated you from the rest of the students. All of you have a history of failing in school. Your learning skills are extremely poor.

That's me.

Your arithmetic and reading skills are way behind the other students. That's me.

Some of you are so slow that you haven't passed any subject areas. That's me.

And then, with a score of 27 out of 100, that would make me absolutely the class flunky. The dumb, dumb. The stupid one. That's me. I couldn't escape it. It was a stigma that would be with me a long, long time.

The next day the teacher requested a meeting with Mom and Pop, and, of course, me.

Jimmy has some learning problems, blah, blah, blah.

We've had problems with Jimmy at St Lucy's, responded Mom. We just don't know what to do with him.

Of course, I wasn't saying anything. I was angry. Angry at Mom and Pop. Angry at Grandpa. Angry at Uncle Victor and Uncle Billy. And angry at the Church.

Now I was in this special class for special help. Help with the three R's. Reading, writing and arithmetic.

With January came more cold and snow. And living in the pigsty was as cold as ever. Just before bed, Mom, Joanie and I would huddle around the upstairs grate, trying to get warm. Standing there I would put on socks and mittens to keep my feet and hands warm. Then I'd make a mad dash to the bed burrowing myself underneath the cold sheets and blankets trying to keep warm, wishing the winter would end.

Eventually the cold and snow did give way to the longer and warmer days of spring. Longer days to play hide and seek outside until Mom called us home.

Can't we stay out and play longer?

No, Jimmy! It's dark and I want you and Joanie in the house now!

All the other Moms are letting their kids stay out.

I said no! I don't care about the other moms!

But why?

Because I said so!

Because I said so, mocking her, underneath my breath. It was her eleventh commandment.

Angry, I shouted at her. I hate this house!

What did I tell you about that kind of talk! I'll wash your mouth out with soap! You should be lucky we have a place to live. You get to bed! Now!

I tuned her out. I didn't care. I was swearing at her underneath my breath. She couldn't see me as I went up the stairs, so I made a nasty gesture to her, knowing that on Saturday I would have to confess, Bless me father for I have sinned. I made a nasty gesture with my finger to my own mother.

On Saturday after confession we went to Aunt Connie's house. When we came home Mom saw the cellar door was opened.

Papa, are you down there? Hearing a groan she went down the cellar. There was a moment of silence then she yelled for Pop.

Jim. Come down here! Hurry up!

A few moments later Pop was carrying Grandpa's small body up the stairs.

What happened to Grandpa Colella?

He fell down the stairs and split open his head. We need to get him to the hospital. See why I don't want you to drink?

I took a deep breath but didn't say anything. I was tired of the arguments.

At school I was struggling even in my new special learning class. Nothing improved. I didn't even try. I didn't care. I just kept thinking about summer, which came and went too quickly and just brought the start of another school year.

It was the same old thing.

Jimmy's behind the other kids in reading and arithmetic. He has poor learning skills. Blah, blah and blah. Jimmy will not pass the school year. So what's the big deal? I flunked elementary school for the third time. Mom and Pop didn't say anything.

On the first day of summer vacation Joanie and I were outside sitting on the front steps with Tippy when Mom and Pop called us in the house.

Kids, we're moving, said Pop.

To where? We both asked at the same time.

Back to Seymour Street.

We didn't say anything. We were just happy.

On the day we moved, shortly before we left, I ran up the backyard stairs to the chicken coop and wrote the words, Jimmy Was Here. But I never told anyone. I came down the stairs and looked at my haven, the grapevines, where Tippy and I would spend time. When I walked out front Tippy was sitting on the front porch stairs. She looked at me as if to say, Why are you going? I hugged and kissed her good-bye. Just as I did that

Mom got out of the car and asked Joanie and I to sit next to Tippy for a picture. Then we hugged her one more time. It would be the last time we saw Tippy. A week later she got hit by a bus and died on the way to the vet. I often go back and look at that picture of her. Tippy was a good friend.

That day was also the last time I ever say my Grandpa or my Colella Uncles. I don't know what happened to them or even how or when they died until recently.

It's also weird, but I don't have any memories of Grandma Colella in that shanty house. I know she did cleaning work at the local theatre to help pay the bills. After all, Grandpa was throwing what little money they had into booze. With thirteen kids in the family, all their money went for food and what little clothing they could afford. I guess that's why they had such a broken down house. They couldn't afford basic living, let alone save any money.

Chapter 18

I was relieved to be back with the Corsos on Seymour Street. At least here I could play with my cousin Johnny. He was two years younger than me so we had lots in common with each other. But what I was most thankful for was to be in a nice, warm, clean house. Delighted to be back in my old bed, rocking myself to sleep.

One day Johnny, Joanie and I were playing hide-and-seek outside after supper. It was good being back into my old neighborhood.

I need to go to the bathroom, yelled Johnny. I'll be right back. He sprinted into the house while Joanie and I waited on the front porch.

A short time later we heard Aunt Louise screaming for Uncle Frankie. We ran into the house and saw Uncle Frankie rushing up the stairs. Johnny was screaming. Mom and Pop rushed upstairs.

What happened? asked Mom.

Johnny put his hand into the rollers on the washing machine!

He did what?

The rollers went all the way up to his elbow! We need to get him to the hospital!

Curiosity must have got the best of him. Wondering what would happen if he put his fingers to the rollers. Not to be outdone, two days later curiosity got the best of me. Mom was washing clothes when I walked into the washroom. With her back to me she didn't hear me come into the room. Quietly standing I watched the rollers spinning. Then deliberately and cautiously I straightened out my right hand and slowly placed the tip of my fingers between the rollers, never thinking the ringers would suck in my middle finger and bring the rest of my hand and wrist along with it into the spinning rollers.

My God, Jimmy, what are you doing? As she frantically unplugged the cord and separated the rollers, she screamed for Pop to help her.

They rushed to me the same hospital and the same doctor as Johnny.

Will he be okay?

Yes, Mrs. Corso. I am curious as to how two boys could possibly do the same stunt within two days of each other. I'm not sure how long it will take his wrist to heal.

My wrist healed, but to this day every time I bend my right wrist down a pointed bone bumps up and reminds me of my little stunt.

Things remained quiet for a week until one morning we were awakened by the sounds of Joanie crying and throwing up. Mom, frightened and panicked as always, was in Joanie's room in a matter of seconds asking her what was wrong.

I don't know. I've felt sick all night. Then I threw up.

Do you feel hot?

Yes. And I have a pain in my side!

Jim, call Dr. Grant! And hurry. And bring the thermometer!

Dr. Grant examined and poked her side. Then took her temperature again.

You need to take her to the hospital right away. I'm pretty sure her appendix is going to burst. I will call them and tell them what is happening.

Am I pregnant?

No, honey, said Mom as the three of them laughed.

I didn't laugh because I didn't know why it was so funny.

Dr. Grant tried to calm Joanie down. You have a bad appendix. It's infected and it needs to come out right away.

Why doesn't Jimmy have it?

Honey, just because he's your twin doesn't mean he'll get the same things as you. Some people never have problems with their appendix. Your mom and dad are going to take you to the hospital. The nurses and doctors are very nice and they will take care of you. You're going to be fine, Joanie.

After Dr. Grant left I asked Mom and Pop what pregnant meant.

We don't have time to talk about it right now, said Mom.

Can't you tell me real fast?

No, Jimmy. We're too busy. Besides, you'll find out for yourself someday.

That was always Pop's standard answer when it came to facts of life.

For most of America, it was the start of the fabulous fifties. It began as a sleepy-time decade and ended with the launching of Sputnik and a revolution in Cuba. It was supposedly the time of solid family life--secure and stable for most families. But our family was far from stable.

The highlight of the 1950s was our T.V. set. We all loved that square box with people inside of it. It was the era of many great Italian singers. Aunt Jenny loved Perry Como and the other Aunts loved Frank Sinatra. But Mom's favorite was always Jerry Vale.

Besides "I Love Lucy," we all liked the "Texaco Star Theatre" and the antics of Imogene CoCo and Sid Caesar on "Your Show of Shows." Radio supposedly was a thing of the past. T.V. was new. It was the future.

A few weeks into the summer Pop asked me if I would like to take accordion lessons.

I guess. Why?

We think it will help you out in school.

How will it do that?

It teaches study habits and discipline. You'll learn to sit down and concentrate on notes. You can take lessons from Paul Ferenza. He has an office on the east side of town.

What about the accordion?

We'll rent one from him.

Okay, shrugging my shoulders.

As for me learning the accordion, that wasn't going to happen. Mr. Ferenza tried to teach me to read sheet music. But I wasn't patient.

Jimmy, you need to sit still and pay attention to me. And stop bouncing your legs up and down.

But I couldn't do it. Towards the end of the summer I told Pop I didn't want to play the accordion.

It takes time, Jimmy. You need to be patient and practice everyday.

I don't want to do it anymore dad. I'm tired of carrying it and lugging it on and off the bus. I hate it!

Give it two more weeks and see what happens.

I gave it two more weeks. Then I quit. I wanted to be out playing, not sitting down trying to learn some notes that made no sense to me. The only thing I did enjoy sitting down and listening to was the Yankees playing baseball. I was a big Yankee fan but none of the Uncles liked them. With the radio on on the back porch I listened to Mel Allen announce the game while I threw a tennis ball against the house and caught it in my glove. Pop and Uncle John walked on the back porch, and Uncle John yelled, Why you like those bums! They stink!

Yeh, how come, Jimmy? said Pop, always supporting his male friends instead of his son.

Because I like them, I said quietly.

71

I hope they get beat, said Uncle John.

Yeh, said Pop, laughing. There was never any foundation between Pop and me. We would always be on opposite sides of in our views of religion, sports and politics.

I didn't say anything else. Instead I walked away from them and retreated into my own little world of daydreaming. It was always the same thing in the family. The males would dominate and overpower the mothers and children with their chauvinistic attitudes.

Going into the house, I passed Mom in her bedroom saying prayers in front of her makeshift altar. She had a statue of the Blessed Mother in the center, draped with her rosary-beads and statue of Saint Joseph and Saint Jude. No matter where we moved she would have the same makeshift altar. Praying for us to arrive safely at our next destination. She prayed five times a day.

The summer was coming to an end. Johnny and I were getting in the last few days of staying out until dark. Having to go to the bathroom, I ran into the house and passed Mom and Pop talking in the kitchen.

Where's Joanie?

I don't know.

Could you please find her? We need to talk to both of you.

Just then Joanie walked into the kitchen.

Where've you been?

Just around. Upstairs. What difference does it make?

Nothing, Joanie. Are you okay?

Yesss, Mom. I'm fine.

Kids, we're moving, blurted out Pop.

I was furious. Now where are we going? We just got here!

Next week we are moving in with Uncle Nick and Aunt Jenny on Marcella Street. You kids will have a nice place to play. It's across the street from Burnett Park.

The only problem is that Joanie and Shirley will have to share a room.

What!? I don't want to share a room. I want my own room!

It'll just be temporary, Joanie, until we get a bigger place to live.

Joanie and I left the kitchen, but we could hear Mom and Pop arguing.

Jim, I tired of living with relatives! And I know they're tired of us living with them! I want my own house with no relatives!

We can't afford not to live with anyone right now! As soon as I get on my feet we'll be able to get our own home!

That's what you always say! How many times have we moved since we've been married? This is not good for the kids! They should have their own house by now!

Damn you, Lena! Why do you always have to be so difficult! The kids will be just fine. They'll have a chance to make new friends. I just need more time to get some money together.

No! You don't understand, Jim! I want my own house with no relatives! That's your life, not mine! I'm tired of it! When's it going to stop?

I keep telling you, as soon as I can get back on my feet and get some money together we'll have our own place. Until then we'll just have to make the best of it.

I said I don't want to live with them!

Damn it, Lena, that's why God never helps you!

Mom went crazy. She picked up a dish and threw it at Pop.

Who do you think you are? Screaming and yelling.

Joanie and I peeked through the door and saw Mom go to the cupboard, get another dish, and throw it at Pop.

Why did you do that? He was laughing at her.

This really angered Mom. She threw all the pots and pans at Pop.

Two days later we moved to Marcella Street.

Chapter 19

So far we had moved six times. From Seymour to Oswego, back to Seymour, then Kingsley, Seymour again, and now Marcella Street. Six moves, five schools.

No wonder I had a nervous stomach and didn't care about school. I just wasn't learning how to function academically and socially.

When we moved from Seymour it was for the last time. It seemed the Corso kids were finally leaving the house that had been our focal point for meetings, arguments, holidays, celebrations of baptisms, first communions, confirmations, birthdays and deaths. Everyone wanted their independence. Everyone either built or bought their own home. Everyone, except Pop.

We went to live with Uncle Nick on Marcella Street. Pop literally couldn't break his family ties. It was part of his dysfunctional life style. And he didn't care what anyone thought, not even Mom.

It was a nice, clean house. Small for seven people, but the seven of us seemed to manage and get along with each other most of the time.

Like on Kingsley, we had to share one bathroom. Joanie was with Shirley, Mom and Pop had their own room, and so did Uncle Nick and Aunt Jenny. My room was a tiny attic with a tiny window that I peered out onto a little backyard with a few old maple trees. I had just enough room for a bed and a small dresser. But I didn't complain. At least I was by myself. But right now I had a bigger problem. Tomorrow was the first day of school. Yuck! It was fall 1950.

My new school was Fraser, and I was repeating second grade, for the second time.

I lumbered into the classroom and found a seat in my favorite spot, the last row in back of the room. I noticed there weren't any inkwells in the desk. The teacher probably took them out because some of the boys would always grab a few strands of hair from the girls in front of them and dip them into the well.

Mrs. Moore, the teacher, introduced herself, and quickly took attendance. Then she immediately separated us into two groups.

She divided us into two learning groups, just like Porter. I assume she had some kind of record about me because I was assigned to go to the next room. No surprise there.

As the weeks passed, she had an assistant work with us on reading and arithmetic skills at a very slow pace. I still could barely read, and I wasn't trying too hard to improve.

We would sit in a circle and take turns reading sentences. Every time it was my turn I would slowly try to pronounce each word, always having difficulty, even the easiest words.

The assistant would ask us what we learned from our reading. Every time she got to me I had difficulty remembering what I read.

Jimmy, can you explain this paragraph?

Squirming in my chair, Ah, well, uhm. No. I just shrugged my shoulders and said nothing.

Every day seemed like a burden. I didn't care about any of the material in class. It was all boring. I just doodled or scribbled on paper.

What are you doing, Jimmy?

Nothing.

I can see that. Why aren't you trying your arithmetic?

I don't understand it.

If you don't try then you'll never understand.

It's too hard.

It's too hard because you don't try.

Who cares about numbers anyways? They're not important.

Look at me, Jimmy. You need arithmetic. You need to know how to make change when you're at the grocery store, the drug store, the gas station and everyday life. Your education is important to you. Nobody can ever take that away from you.

The next day while scarfing down my supper, Mom told me she had gotten a phone call from Mrs. Moore.

Yeh, so?

She said you're not trying on your schoolwork.

So?

Don't so us, young man! She said you're not trying at all.

I don't understand that stuff.

What stuff?

All that reading and questions she asks. And why is arithmetic so important? You told us you never passed sixth grade. Then you dropped out of school!

And I always told you, times were different. We had a big family. I had to help around the house while Grandma and Grandpa went to work.

I graduated from Vocational High School, said Pop, taking a swallow of wine.

Great! So what did it do for you?

I learned a lot of different skills for working. I can do carpentry, and...

Then I'll learn what you did!

That's okay, Jimmy. But going to school and getting an education is still import. . .

Yeh, yeh! I already heard that from Mrs. Moore!

Do we have any coffee, babe? We're just trying to help you, Jimmy.

I watched Mom as she went to the stove and poured Pop his coffee then placed the cup in front of him. Always catering to his needs, whether she liked it or not.

Do we have any cream?

Again, like a trained animal, she went to the refrigerator and got his cream.

You need to try harder. You've been slow since kindergarten.

School is too hard!

You have some learning problems. That's why the teacher separated you from the rest of the class. You can work at a slower pace than the rest of the kids.

The teacher wants us to do some reading with you, said Pop, gulping down another cup of coffee. I'll get you a book

What kind of a book? eyeing him suspiciously.

I'll think of something. I'll see what I can find that you might like.

We'll read with you after supper. That means no T.V., said Mom, as she poured Pop another cup of coffee.

Reading slow. Arithmetic worse. Just another school year. All I'm thinking is what happened to summer vacation? How could it go by so fast? Come on, Christmas vacation!

But Mom at least tried, for a while. There we were. The inept leading the inept. One didn't make it past sixth grade. The other couldn't make it past second grade. One never read a book. The other didn't know how to read a book. We both sputtered and tried to pronounce the words. Mom trying to help. But the words were just as difficult for her and as they were for me.

This book is hard, Mom. Why can't dad help us with these words?

He doesn't have time. He works all day. When he gets home he's too tired to help you. He deserves to rest at the end of the day.

But he knows how to say all these words and what they mean. That's all he does when he comes home is eat supper then sit in front of the T.V. until bedtime. Besides, how long will it take to help me? Fifteen minutes from his T.V. time?

And what was that magical book that Pop got for me that would turn around my fortunes and make me a better reader and learner in school? Of all the books available for kids to read, he got me a book on how to repair television sets. Television sets! I couldn't believe it. I know my teachers never knew that. I would read alone at night in bed, not after supper with them. I read about picture tubes, transistors and other parts that absolutely didn't make any sense. It was frustrating to read the book. I didn't hate reading it. I just wished it were easier.

The autumn leaves were changing into the spectacular colors of late fall. I spent after school time walking in Burnett Park looking at the trees and flowers or throwing the tennis ball against the house and catching it.

Sometimes on Saturday Johnny would come over the house to play baseball. Although two years younger, he was already taller than me and could hit the ball farther. When it was my turn to hit the ball to Johnny it landed in the neighbor's front yard that was surrounded by a white picket fence.

Crap!

What's the matter?

Did you see where the ball landed?

Yeh. So what's the big deal? We'll just knock on the door and ask to get it.

You don't understand. Those people are jerks. They have a daughter who must be in twelfth grade. Last week I saw her beat the heck out of one of the neighbor girls. She's mean.

We approached the front door slowly and nervously rapped on the door. I stood there crossing my legs as if I had to go to the bathroom. Just as I feared, the daughter opened the door.

We. . .we hit the ball in your front yard. Can we please get it?

No! You little brats! You should've thought about that before you hit the ball! Now get the hell out of here!

We better go, I whispered to Johnny. I'll try to get it another time.

The next day I was walking by her house and saw the ball lying on the ground next to some bushes. Thinking she was not at home, I jumped the fence. Before I could clear the fence on my way out, she had me by the arm. She pulled me around toward her and slapped me so hard that I got a large red welt on the right side of my face.

I told you, stay out of my yard, you little brat! She grabbed the ball from me and headed back to the house.

If I catch you in this yard again, I'll give you twice the licking.

God, I wanted to belt her. I didn't care if she was a girl. I never said anything to anyone. At supper that night I kept my head down, hoping Mom wouldn't see my face, but she did. She walked over to me, not saying a word, and raised my head.

You been fighting again, haven't you?

I knew you would say that!

What did I tell you about fighting!

I wasn't fighting!

Then why do you have that red mark on your face!

I was wrestling with some of the guys down the street.

What did I tell you about fighting!? And she slapped me on my arm for the umpteenth time.

Chapter 20

Fall gave way to another harsh, cold, winter, but it also meant Christmas vacation. As was the Corso tradition, on Christmas day we all gathered together on Seymour Street for lots of food and gifts.

Grandma would make her homemade spaghetti. She would bring the long noodles into her bedroom and place them on a clean bed sheet so they would dry and be ready for supper. When the spaghetti was dry she would cook it and serve it with tomato sauce with breadcrumbs over it, along with homemade meatballs and sausages.

Always wearing her familiar flowered apron, she would take out a large pot and toss in live snails. Jokingly she said the ones that crawled the fastest were the ones we'll cook and eat. After they were cooked, we would scoop them out of their shells using a toothpick and then stir them in hot melted butter making a yummy treat.

We also had baccala--fish dishes, calamari and squid. Hot Italian breads were split in half and smothered in butter and olive oil. We had mashed and sweet potatoes, bananas, apples, oranges, cherries, pears, tangerines, pomegranates, and it was all topped off with cannoli.

Eating meals at these large family gatherings was never dull. Discussion was always religion, politics, and sports.

Hey, Rocky, you think DiMaggio should have retired?

I think he made a mistake, Sam. He should have retired last year.

What difference does that make? What's important is that he's an Italian who hit in 56 straight games, said Uncle Joey, fiercely proud of his heritage.

What's even more amazing is that he spent time in the service, said Uncle Nick.

I hate the Yankees! blurted out Uncle Joe. I wanted to say something but I just remained silent. It would be a waste of time defending the Yankees against the Uncles.

Can anybody tell me what's happening in Korea?

We're going to war, Lena, and I don't want to go back again, said Uncle Joey.

Why does there have to be another war? Wasn't one war enough?

Apparently not, Lena. Where is Korea?

I think it's in Europe.

I thought it was in Asia.

I thought it was South America.

Who cares where it is? It's none of our business.

And, even though no one knew very much about it, the war conversation continued the next several minutes. This was followed by several minutes of lively discussion on who would be the next President of the country.

While the men were debating politics, the women, as was the custom, cleared the tables then washed and dried the dishes. The ladies then brought in two large trays of cannoli and two pots of coffee. The discussion then turned to movie stars like Elizabeth Taylor, Clark Gable, and Bogart.

Suddenly it became quiet. That more or less was the signal that there was nothing left to talk about.

I guess I'll go into the parlor and sit on the sofa.

I'm with you, Jim.

Me too. All the Uncles got up and went into the parlor while the women finished working in the kitchen.

In the parlor the Uncles and Pop, as was the custom in the family, took a short nap.

The next week we visited Aunt Connie's for New Year's Eve dinner. After dinner we left and started home. But Pop wanted to go to Seymour Street to be with the family.

Let's go to Ma's house, babe, so we can celebrate New Year's there.

Yeh! Let's go, I said. It'll be fun.

No! I don't want to go! I'm tired of being around them!

But it will be fun, Mom!

I said I don't want to go!

Please! Everybody is going to be there!

I guess that made her mad because she turned around and gave me her customary slaps on the arm. I don't want to be near them! Don't you understand that?

Tired of getting slapped on the arm, I retreated again into my little world and remained silent.

Mom and Pop kept arguing back and forth.

Why do they always have to end up fighting? whispered Joanie.

I just shrugged my shoulders and didn't say anything. We loathed them for arguing so much.

Why do you have to get like that, Lena?

Under my breath, I'm saying, Yeh, Mom, why are you always acting like this? Why do you spoil everything? Why can't you be happy?

Why do we have to always be with them for the holidays? We were just there last week for Christmas.

New Year's is supposed to be fun, Lena. It's no fun unless we celebrate it with family.

Finally, under Pop's persistent pressure, Mom gave in and we headed to Seymour Street.

When we arrived everyone was already in a good mood. We all milled around until midnight. As the final minutes got near, Shirley turned up the radio and we listened to Guy Lombardo and his band saying the final countdown. Uncle Joey grabbed a pot and put it over his head, while Uncle Joe grabbed a frying pan and a wooden spoon and banged them together. We all joined in for the final countdown and yelled Happy New Year. The men then filled their shot glasses with clear liquid Anisette. Yuck! They raised and touched the glasses and said Happy New Year.

Everybody was hugging and kissing. We all laughed as Uncle Rocky did his two-legged shuffle, which he did only on special occasions.

Everyone was having a good time, except Mom. She was sitting in the corner of the room, arms folded, legs crossed, not laughing or smiling. Just a sad face.

Why can't she be happy? Why does she always have to be so difficult? Maybe Pop is right. That's why God doesn't help her.

Chapter 21

The winter months went by slowly. To get through those months we all escaped by watching T.V.—"The Colgate Comedy Hour," "The Lone Ranger," "Kraft Television," "Your Hit Parade," "I Love Lucy," and "You Bet Your Life," with one of my favorite funny men, Groucho Marx.

School was there but nothing else. But now I just kept thinking about Easter vacation. I was still struggling with my reading. I might have wanted to do better, but I really didn't care.

You need to try harder, said Pop. It's important that you do your best.

If you don't learn to read and write you will grow up to be a bum and dig ditches.

Yeh, I know, Mom. You told me a thousand times.

So I worked on my reading, even with the television repair book, because I didn't want to grow up and be a bum and dig ditches.

The winter turned into March. It was a cold, snowy day and I was sitting at my desk doodling while the rest of the special education students were doing their work.

Hi, Jimmy. How are you doing today?

I looked up, and it was Mrs. Moore with some lady I didn't know.

Fine. I shrugged my shoulders and went back to doodling.

Mrs. Moore bent down and gently touched my hand, which actually had a soothing effect on me.

Jimmy, this is Mrs. Wilcox. She's a district psychologist. She would like to talk to you. Is that okay?

I guess. Shrugging my shoulders, but still doodling. Why?

Jimmy, I've seen your transcript. You haven't done well in regular class. You struggled in special education at Porter, and now you're struggling in special education here.

A lot of kids don't do good in school.

That's true, but you're way below the other kids. In fact, Jimmy, you're the lowest in the class. You have severe learning problems. Learning is very difficult for you.

I guess I don't like school.

I would like to give you a series of tests.

What for?

The tests will help us understand your learning skills.

Will they make me a better reader and do better in school?

No, they won't, but it they will help us to determine what your problem is, and then we can structure things for your learning. We really need to test you, Jimmy.

Okay, if you think it will help me.

I took the tests but the questions seemed stupid. I kept asking myself why I needed to be evaluated by a psychologist. God, I wish spring vacation would hurry up and get here.

Then, much to my delight, it finally was spring. On a beautiful Saturday morning Johnny and I were playing baseball at Burnett Park, surrounded by large trees, several flowerbeds, a swimming pool, baseball fields, tennis courts and other activity fields.

But what got my attention on that day were the beautiful trees and flowers. Two of the flowers I knew--tulips and roses. Walking around the flowerbed I saw how the sun cast a shadow over some the flowers making them appear sad and droopy. Jimmy, keep your head up and a smile on your face. And walk straight. Don't droop your shoulders.

And yet some of the flowers were straight. Like they were standing making them appear bright and happy. Why can't Mom be happy? It's almost as if their beautiful colors acted as their souls. Mom talked about the soul. The nuns talked about the soul. And the priests are always talking about the soul. It was easier to see the soul of a flower.

I stopped and looked at the tulips. Some closed. Others open. For a brief moment I have a euphoric feeling like everything is good and beautiful in the world. But the feeling quickly fades.

I'm brought back to reality by the voices of Johnny and Joanie calling me to play that familiar game, what does this cloud look like? The cloud could be an animal, a plant or tree or anything our imaginations wanted it to be.

The next week Mom and Pop received a letter from the school asking them to call Mrs. Wilcox to discuss my tests results.

What test results? asked Mom.

I don't know. She came to the classroom last week with Mrs. Moore and asked me if I would like to take some tests.

Why?

I don't know. She said it might help me to do better in school.

Why weren't we told about this test? Pop was already on the phone calling the school.

How would I know? I thought you knew.

Pop was talking with Mrs. Wilcox. I didn't stay to listen to what they were saying. Instead I went outside to play. The next day after school Mrs. Wilcox cornered me at the top of the stairwell.

Come into my office, Jimmy, so we can discuss your evaluation. I followed to her office.

This visit would change my life forever.

She had brown eyes and short brown hair. Wearing a white ruffled blouse and a tan skirt and jacket, she put her briefcase on top of the desk and asked me to be seated.

How would you like to go to another school next year?

Why? Although I already had a pretty good idea what she was going to say. I'd heard it all before. Jimmy, you're slow and have difficulty learning, and blah, blah, blah.

Jimmy your test scores were extremely low. You. . .

So? I blurted out, not giving her a chance to finish.

You're slow, Jimmy, and you need special help in school.

I've already been getting special help. I've been in the special room with other students since last year.

This is different, Jimmy. I talked to your dad on the phone but asked him not to say anything to you until I talked to you first. This school has a special education class for students who have serious learning problems like you. I have contacted this school and talked to them about the class. They have hired a new teacher who specializes in working with special education students. She's a young teacher that just graduated from Syracuse University. Because of your slow learning skills, your parents, Mrs. Moore and I all feel that this is in your best interest. You need to transfer to Seymour School. Do you know where.

That's where I used to live!

Then you know the area?

Yeh. It's right down the street from my Grandma's house.

You'll really like this school Jimmy. Are you willing to give it a try?

I guess.

Good. It's a great opportunity for you to improve your learning skills. And I know you will like this class. It'll be fun for you.

But inside I'm thinking, there's no such thing as having fun in school or even liking school.

Do you have any questions?

No.

I'll talk to your Mom and Dad about making arrangements for next year.

I walked out of her office thinking, what's the big deal? To me, it's just another stupid school year. To her, Mrs. Moore and Mom and Pop it seemed like the magical answer.

Yes, Mom, she talked to me today at school. I scarfed down a sausage at the supper table. She said I was going to Seymour School next year.

You know you scored a 70 on your test.

So. What does that mean?

It means you have to be in special education class for kids who are extremely slow. That will be good for you, Jimmy. You're slow and behind in your arithmetic and reading skills. Besides you'll be close to grandma's house. We can pick you up after. . .

Mom, I know! I'm slow! Mrs. Moore says I'm slow. Mrs. Wilcox says I'm slow. You guys say I'm slow, so I guess I'm slow!

You don't need to be sarcastic. We're just trying to help you.

How will I get there?

I'll drive you there the first few days. After that you can walk home. It's only a half-hour walk from the house.

I ate the rest of my supper in silence then left the kitchen. From the parlor I could hear them talking to Uncle Nick and Aunt Jenny.

What does that score mean?

We don't really know, Nick. But Mrs. Wilcox seems to think it's pretty bad.

These new tests don't always mean anything.

Mrs. Wilcox said anything below 70 is considered retarded.

That doesn't sound like Jimmy. He doesn't act retarded.

You're right, Jen, but we don't know that. We have to go on the advice of Mrs. Wilcox and the teacher. There's nothing we really can do. Pop belched. He has to go to Seymour. He's already been in special class for nearly two years, and God knows he still hasn't done anything in school. Maybe this will help him.

Nothing was said to me the rest of the school year. I didn't ask, nor did I care. To me it was just another school. My sixth school in six years. Right now I have a more pressing need. How can I keep my sanity until summer vacation?

Then, Hallelujah! School's finally out. Thank God. Walking out of school, I kicked over some trashcans, singing that old familiar tune--No more paper, no more books, no more teachers' dirty looks. The happiest time of the year is here! Summer vacation! No school and, most importantly, no stupid teachers giving stupid tests. But in the back of my mind, I'm thinking, I still don't have any skills. I'm still behind the other students. I still need special help. And this fall I will be starting at another school with my three best friends--I'm slow, I don't care and I don't like myself.

I was the classic example of the self-fulfilling prophecy. People kept telling me, Jimmy, you are slow in school, slow in math, slow in reading. Eventually I gave up and just believed it.

The rest of the summer was a typical 50's summer, easy going and lazy except when Joanie and I had to get tested for T.B. Mom and the doctors were concerned that we might get it so we had to get that scratch test with the needle.

Joanie and I might have been enjoying summer, but Mom sure wasn't. Her mental condition was getting worse. Many things were contributing to her state of mind. Worrying about Joanie, living with the relatives, her relationship with Grandma, moving so many times, Pop's inability to pay the bills, and now her little Jimmy Boy was diagnosed as being retarded. She seemed so sad and distant.

But us kids had lots of fun times. Johnny, Joanie and I loved to catch lightning bugs. On those hot summer nights everyone would be out on the back porch escaping the stifling heat. Grabbing jars, the three of us ran around trying to catch those little black bugs that had yellow and red spots on them. I was fascinated by them. What did they have inside them that made them light up at dusk and go off at dawn?

Does anyone know why they light?

You need to ask God, said Mom.

I should have known better than to ask the question. It was the standard answer.

The next day the three of us decided to go to the movie show at the Cameo Theater. It was a double feature. But that meant we had to ask Pop for money, which we hated to do because he always complained about it.

How much do you need?

It's twenty-five cents for each of us.

Twenty-five cents! I can remember when it was a nickel! Money doesn't grow on trees!

Grudgingly he gave us three quarters.

We walked back into the kitchen where Mom was making some Popsicles for us for after the show. She emptied a package of Kool-Aid into a bowl, with sugar, hot water, then cold water. Then she poured the mixture into metal ice trays adding a toothpick to each cube and placed it into the freezer.

The movies always started out with a newsreel about current events, such as the Korean War, followed by sports news, then usually two cartoons. We saw the first movie with Bud Abbott and Lou Costello. The second feature was my favorite group of guys, Leo Gorcey, Huntz Hall and the Bowery boys. All this for twenty-five cents!

On the way home we took our time and watched some little kids playing Red Rover. Further down the street some other kids were playing Red Light, Green Light. Turning the corner and heading up the hill to the house we saw a group of boys playing Kick the Can.

Yep, these were the lazy days of summer. No cares. No problems. But summers come to an end. The start of another dreaded school year. Stupid student at stupid Seymour School.

Chapter 22

It was an adjustment just trying to be in a room with all the different types of "special" kids, especially the really bad off kids. I never knew how to treat them, let alone what they were thinking. As for the class bullies, I avoided them as much as possible. And I also had to deal with the "regular" kids in the school. They would snicker and laugh at us or make comments when we were in the hall. They even made fun of the eyes of the Down's Syndrome kids and the way epileptic Earl walked.

I'm with the misfits, Joanie. I'm the youngest kid in a class of misfits.

That's not true, Jimmy.

Yes it is. Look at the kids that are in my class.

But they're in there for special help.

Yeh! But you don't have those kinds of kids in your classes, Joanie. You don't have to deal with kids making fun of you. Teasing you when you go down the hall. You don't have to listen to their stupid comments.

Like what?

About being retarded.

But Jimmy, you...

Or there goes the dummies. The retards. Do you think that's fun?

Of course not. But you just have to ignore them.

That's what everybody says.

The stigma of being in this class was bothering me. True, we were different. But I still thought I was different from them, but it was getting harder to tell how. My fate was sealed in that special education class for a long time.

After a couple of months Miss Towne had some idea what we could, or rather what we couldn't, do. After all, she wasn't working with the cream of the crop. She was working with kids who for one reason or another couldn't function in a traditional classroom--learning disabled, physically disabled, emotional problems, behavioral problems. Different ages. We were all in there together.

For most of the students there would be nothing after we left Seymour. Maybe one or two would go to some type of trade school to learn carpentry. But most dropped out of school at sixteen and eventually went into the service, found a job, or ended up on the streets.

Miss Towne worked as best as she could with us, showing extreme patience with the mentally and physically disabled students. I don't see how she kept from mentally falling apart. If she wasn't taking care of Earl during one of his seizures, she was keeping the boys who were behavioral problems from killing each other. Her biggest problem was Chucky. Trying to make sure he didn't pick a fight or dominate the class.

At times some of the kids acted like animals in a zoo. She held her ground. Standing tall, firm and proud. Never losing her composure. Never letting the kids get the best of her.

We will act like young ladies and gentlemen, she would say when students weren't showing proper respect.

As inner city kids, some of us were rejects who didn't care about rules or conformity. But she demanded we show respect to her and each other.

Today, were discussing current events. It's important we understand what is happening in the world.

Moans and groans. The classical response from deadbeat kids that don't care.

Why should we learn anything? Isn't it easier to be stupid? laughed Chucky.

Why do we have to do this? squeaked Liz.

Who cares what's happening in the world? shouted Eddie.

The world's none of our business! blurted Maybel. Who ironically always had her nose in everybody else's business.

The comments didn't bother Miss Towne. She could have become angry. She could have said, Because I said so. Or, You're learning this whether you like it or not. Or, Okay, if that's how you feel, then stay in your seats and do nothing until lunchtime. Or, she could have handed out some paper and pencils and had us write why current events are important. But she knew it wouldn't be the right approach. She knew a gentle approach was the best way to work with us.

Being angry would only add fuel to the fire. The kids who caused trouble loved a conflict, hoped for a conflict, wanted a conflict. But they didn't get one because she knew that is what they wanted. She also knew most of the kids couldn't do the assignments. They had difficulty reading and most couldn't even write a complete sentence. A gentle approach using class discussion and answering the kids in a respectful manner would get the best results.

Who's the president of the United States?

I knew the answer but didn't say anything. How many times has Pop talked about Truman? Always proclaiming he will go down in history as one of the great presidents of this country.

Truman, said one voice.

Good. Now who can tell me the vice president?

Silence. No one knew who he was.

Has anyone ever heard of Alben Barkley? Well, he's our vice president. What about Korea? she asked.

What about it? laughed Tony, in a smart-ass voice. He was the sneak in the class. Always doing things behind Miss Towne's back. Making sure he never got caught.

Where is Korea? She walked over to the side table and picked up a globe and pointed to a spot that nobody knew

It's located in Asia, on the Sea of Japan. How is the country divided?

Again no one answers. We certainly were not up on current events.

It's divided into two countries. North and South. Which side are we supporting?

Again I knew the answer, but I didn't want to say anything because I might embarrass myself. Besides Chucky and the guys might laugh at me.

South! says a voice from the back of the room.

North! says another voice.

It's south, stupid!

Don't call me stupid! You ass!

I'm calling you stupid. So what are you going to do bout it? I didn't have to turn around to see who was calling the other kid stupid. I knew who it was.

In a matter of seconds, Miss Towne is in the back of the room. But her quickness is no match for Chuck's quickness. He leaps the desk in one step. His right fist pummels the middle of Tony's face giving him a bloody nose. Tony yells and gives him the All-American salute with that middle finger and tells him to kiss his ass. Before Tony can retaliate Miss Towne is between them.

I won't tolerate this kind of behavior, Chuck! Nor will I tolerate that kind of language, Tony! We will act like young gentlemen! Chuck, you go to the other side of the room, and Tony, you sit down and keep quiet.

Chucky could have cared less what she thought. No need for him to play by the rules. Rules are for sissies and a sissy he wasn't. His thing was disobeying orders. To bully, control and dominate. I thought he should join the Army or Marines. They would knock that chip off his shoulder.

A few minutes later Miss Towne was back in the front of the classroom. Unfazed by what happened, she said, Let's talk about sports.

Raymond blurted out, Did you know you can buy Topps baseball cards with bubble gum in them? Yeh, see right here! He spread some cards on his desk.

I've put them on the spokes of my bike with a clothespin. They make a neat sound.

Who cares about sports cards? They're not important anyways! yelled Eddie.

Across the room Virginia raised her hand.

Yes, Virginia?

There is a new program on T.V.

What's it about?

I think she was happy that we were at least responding to questions, even though it wasn't exactly what she had in mind. At least we were participating and involved in class discussion.

It's this lady who does crazy things and she is married to a guy from another country with an accent. And I think its gonna be on T.V. tonight.

Oh yea, said another voice. It's called "I Love Lucy." And it's real funny.

After a few minutes of this, Miss Towne sensed that we were losing interest so she gave us some activity time.

This time was meant for us to socialize and interact with each other for social development. But the by-product was one clique taunting another clique. Sarcasm, and rudeness we understood. It was part of our nature. Politeness, courtesy, and respect were something Miss Towne was trying to teach us.

Ranging in age from 9 to 14, with low self-esteem and poor academic skills, we had been pulled out of regular class and placed into special education in hopes that it would do something for our mental and social development. Miss Towne certainly didn't have an enviable job.

After the activity time Miss Towne called us together for a talk about classroom behavior. People, part of my job is working on proper behavior and social skills. We need to learn to respect one another. We can't settle our differences by fists. Fighting gets you nowhere. We also need to learn life skills, such as brushing our teeth to prevent cavities and bad breath and taking a bath for body cleanliness and so we don't smell.

Are we going to do anything else besides classroom stuff? asked Virginia.

Yes, we are. I have arranged a field trip to visit the zoo at Burnett Park. Also, we will be going on a field trip to the bakery at the end of the block. And we will be taking a bus trip to downtown to one of the local stores so we can learn how to use tokens and behave in public.

Everything she taught us was for practical purposes for day-to-day living.

Academically it was even more difficult for her. We were so diversified in our backgrounds that there was basically no chance of us being on the same level. She gave us workbooks to mark our progress, but even that was on a limited level. The class had to be structured more for everyday survival skills than for academics. Miss Towne was a very special teacher. She did the best she could, especially considering it was the dark ages for special need students.

Chapter 23

Chucky didn't like me. Not that I cared. I just didn't want him to kill me.

I walked to the back of the room. He shadowed me. He intentionally bumped into me hoping to provoke a fight.

Why'd you do that?

Because I wanted to! His gruff voice taking pleasure in what he did. I don't like you, Corso!

That's too bad! Not backing down from him.

I'll see you after school! His eyes filled with pleasure.

Talking to him was no solution. I had one possible plan. I would try out running him after school on my way to Grandma's house.

The 3:00 bell rang. I scurried down the stairs as fast as my little legs could run, but not fast enough for him not to see me. He was in hot pursuit hoping to crush my body. Being three years older, he was bigger and stronger. My fast little legs gave way to his stronger body. At the grocery store, a block from Grandma's house, it came to a violent conclusion. As always, I was on the wrong end.

He was like Hercules, with me the proverbial sacrificial lamb. I never had a chance as he pulverized me into a doormat.

Crap, why is it always me? His eyes were shining with delight and hatred. I felt the vibration of my back as he slammed me against the store wall. His arms were like iron as his right hand gave me a blow to the side of my head, knocking me silly. I desperately tried to get under him by putting my head in his stomach and my arms around his waist, only to have him turn me over like a feather. He hit me again. This time I went limp. His strength was no match for me. My nose was bleeding, and I was trying to bite him, but I didn't have enough strength to get my teeth into his hand, arm, or anywhere else on his body. He was ready to strike another blow to my face when I saw a large shadow grab his arms and pull him off me. But not before his right foot smashed into my side, all the while yelling, I--don't—like—you--Corso.

Why don't you pick on someone your own size? The shadow screamed. What's the matter with you? Get out of here!

Are you okay, Jimmy?

Yeh. I recognized him as the owner of the grocery store.

Who's this nut, Jimmy?

He's a kid in my class.

He's in your class! Has he done this before?

He's been picking on me.

Did you tell your teacher?

No. It will just make more trouble.

Do your folks know?

No. I don't want them to know.

You should tell them or your teacher.

No. Everything we'll be fine. Please don't say anything to them. It'll only upset Mom. And dad won't care. He always says I need to fight my own battles.

Okay, but I don't understand. Now you better get home and clean yourself up.

I limped off towards Grandma's house crying and angry at everybody. I hated being small and I wouldn't forgive Chucky no matter what the priests say.

When I got to Grandma's house I quickly sneaked into bathroom and scrubbed my face and arms, hoping Mom wouldn't see any marks on my face. Then I walked home to Marcella Street.

At supper of course Mom asked me about my face, but I just told her I was wrestling at school.

The next day at school I hid behind my books as much as possible hoping no one would ask questions about my face.

I went to extremes not to be near Chucky or have eye contact with him.

At reading time we were placed into groups of four or five, with the better readers in charge of the group. Suddenly I was a group leader. My pronunciation was getting better. My reading skills were slowly improving. Not great, but improving, and certainly much better than most of the kids in my class. My group consisted of Earl, one of the Down's Syndrome kids, A kid named Tommy, and a shy, silent, withdrawn girl named Mary. The book we were reading? *Peter Pan.*

Tommy was the first to read. He pointed to each word and pronounced it very slowly, even the simple words, such as *a* or *the*.

"In a qu..Ie..t stre..Et in Lon...D..on , London, liv..ed t..He DaR...ling fam..ily.

I listened patiently, knowing what he was going through, but no longer needing to point my finger at each word.

The...re Wen...Dy to..ld wo...Wo...der..ful st..oR..ies, said Mary, who was reading just like Tommy, but she was so quiet the group could hardly hear her. Finally, everyone in the group had a turn until we completed two pages.

After reading, we did crafts, such as art, or made things for the coming Christmas season.

As the 3:00 bell rang, I wasn't sure if I should hurry up and run out of the room or lag behind so Chucky wouldn't be at liberty to use me again as his punching bag. But to my surprise and delight he hurried quickly out of the room, losing himself in the hallway among the masses of kids who were anxious to get out of school.

Being in no hurry, I stayed behind and talked to Miss Towne then started home. When I headed out the back gate of the school to Seymour Street, there he was. But to my amazement he was with a girl, who obviously was too old for this school. They were holding hands and kissing. She must be hurting for boys. What in the world could she possibly see in him? What a pair! The beauty and the beast!

Ironically, Chuck never said anything about the fight. Maybe he had his satisfaction or his revenge. We never spoke or acknowledged each other. I avoided him in school and on field trips. He had his victory. I had my defeat.

Chapter 24

The next several weeks went by slowly, but it finally arrived. Christmas vacation! On Christmas day the family gathered at our central meeting place, Grandma's house. As usual everybody was in a festive mood, hugging, laughing and exchanging gifts. It was the early fifties and most of the family was experiencing a time of middle class materialism. New homes, new cars, and a new found independence from each other. There was the usual discussion about politics, sports, religion. Aunt Jenny was talking about S&H Green stamps and Donnie and Shirley were discussing the movie, "The Day the Earth Stood Still."

That's a horror film!

No it's not, Aunt Lena, said Shirley, laughing. It was a fun film.

Do you kids still do those drills in case when we get bombed?

Yeh, Uncle Sam. We do, said Joanie. They make us walk single file down a hallway away from the windows. We sit down on the floor and place our head on our knees and our hands over our head to protect ourselves in case anything falls on our head.

What about those bomb shelters being built in some back yards?

What about them, Uncle Gus? Do we need them? Will they protect us?

What good would they do if we get bombed? Radiation will be in the air a long time. I don't see any purpose for them.

You're probably right, Shirley, and how long can we stay inside one of those things? And how do you go to the bathroom? asked Mom.

As the conversation ended about bomb shelters, the discussion turned to the mafia. Al Capone deserved what he got. He's no hero of the Italian people. Just like Mussolini, he got what he deserved.

The Mafia has no place in this country, said Uncle Joey. They give us Italians a bad name. Most of us work hard, pay our taxes and many of us served in the war.

The newspapers can't use the term Mafia anymore, said Uncle Gus. They have to use the term La Costra Nostra.

The discussions finally ended with the men heading into the parlor. Sitting in sofas and chairs, they unbuckled their belts, laid their heads back, and in the tradition of the family, took a nap.

Me? I was trying to be easy going and happy, but it was hard. I was moody and had wide swings of emotions. Happy to quiet and then to isolation. Cycling myself for weeks, days and months. Mom and Pop fighting and school being what it was, I tried to avoid situations that would put me at odds with anyone. Whether at home, in the car, or at a relative's house, Mom and Pop would fight with each other, causing me to get that nervous, sick feeling.

Christmas week, as always, went by all too fast. The family gathered together to celebrate the New Year. It's twelve o'clock! Happy New Year, 1952.

The new semester was temporarily peaceful with me establishing some friendships, making it bearable to go to school. As for Chucky's gang, they never accepted me. So who cares?

Another cold and bitter upstate New York winter turned into another spring, making me happy. I was tired of the forty-five minute walk home from school that seemed like an eternity for an eleven year old, especially during the winter months. Everyday. Before school and after school. Buckling those goulashes. Walking through snow, slush and cold.

One day I was complaining at supper about the walk when Pop went into one of his lectures. We had it hard in our day. You kids have it easy today.

We had to walk five miles, regardless of the weather, said Uncle Nick.

Yeh! continued Pop. Grandma had to cover the holes in our shoes with newspaper and we never complained one bit. She had to use a darning foot to sew our socks because we couldn't afford to buy socks, let alone shoes.

Yeh, yeh, yeh, I'm thinking to myself, tired of listening to Pop. I certainly don't want to hear it. They always exaggerated the way things really were. So you guys had it tough. Today is today and yours are the old days. So get over it and spare me the lecture. Save the stories for your grandkids. It'll give you something to talk about when you're really old and gray. Of course, I made sure I didn't say any of that out loud to them.

Chapter 25

With spring came the traditional sports and hobbies for elementary school kids. Walking out of the back entrance one day after school, I saw several boys gathered in a circle. I recognized two of the boys from Mrs. Dunham's Social Studies class. I was a little apprehensive about approaching them, but desperately wanted to play with them. It was springtime and boys all over the country were ready to shoot. An old game played by Egyptian and Roman children before the time of Christ.

Hesitatingly, I approached the boys. As I got near them, one of the boys recognized me and said hi. I took this as a sign of acceptance.

Hi. Can I play?

Yeh, if you can find a stick so we can make the circle. Happy they were letting me play, I fetched the stick like a puppy eager to please his master.

Okay, Jimmy, draw a circle and two straight lines across from each other, and make sure that both lines touch the circle.

There were six boys and each took out their bags and gave two marbles, called commies, to one of the boys who put them in the circle. Using one of his own marbles, he placed it in the center and then placed three marbles, called object marbles or commies, on each side of the center marble, forming a cross.

Okay, let's play! said Anthony.

We knuckled down on the ground at the pitch line and were allowed one shot for lagging to see who would go first and start the most popular game of marbles called

Ringer. We were playing for keeps, which meant that a player keeps the marbles he shoots out of the ring. The secret was being able to hold the shooter between your forefinger and thumb, and then flick it just right so you could have a good shot.

I'll go first, said Mickey, using his shooter which we called a Monny trying to get as close as he could to the lag line. But he was only a little halfway past the center of the circle.

I went next. But my shooter landed in the middle of the circle. Not much skill there.

The next two boys shot farther but still weren't close to the lag line.

The fifth boy named Anthony shot his marble.

Wow, great shot, Anthony! I said. As his marble landed a few inches from the lag line.

The last boy shot his marble but landed behind me, making me feel good because I didn't have the worst shot.

Anthony shot first because he was closest to the lag line. His shot hit and knocked one of the marbles out of the cross and the ring.

Good shot! I said again, trying to build him up and hoping I could be on the good side of the gang.

His next shot hit a marble but fell short of going inside the circle.

The other boys shot in order, each hitting a marble but not knocking it out of the ring.

It was my turn to shoot again, but I didn't hit any marbles. Still not much skill there.

They each went around several more times with Anthony having four marbles. Three more and he wins the game.

You can't do that! said Anthony, talking to the boy who shot after me.

I'm not doing anything.

Yes, you are. Your hand is across the ring line. You can't do that.

It's not across the ring line, it's on it, and that's fair.

No, it's not fair either.

It was called Hunching, and it wasn't fair. Nor was Histing, when a player raises his hand from the ground when shooting.

They were arguing back and forth but I didn't care. It was only a game of marbles but some of the boys took seriously. We finished the game with Anthony winning.

Hey Corso, what grade you in?

I'm in Miss Towne's class. I avoided saying special education.

So what does she teach?

He must have been a new student. Everyone in the building knows where the special education room is. God knows how much the kids make fun of us.

He's in special education class, said Johnny. The class for slow kids. You know, the retarded kids?

I glared at him, taking offense at, the remark. Swallowing my pride and hoping they would still accept me, I kept quiet not wanting to provoke any kind of disagreement.

Hey, isn't there a kid named Chuck in that class? I saw him in a fight after school one day. He must be the toughest kid in school.

I knew what he meant but didn't want to say anything.

See ya later! We separated at the gate to go home. I was hoping they would let me be a part of their little group.

Yeh, said Anthony.

Walking down the street, I felt good about being allowed to play, but thought about the comments of being slow and retarded. I'd heard the comments many times before when walking down the hall. It was obvious our class was different. Anybody could see that. This was a "special education" class, not a mainstream class. But what angered me the most was when some of the kids called us dummies.

When I got home I heard Shirley and Joanie yelling.

Don't you yell at me, Joanie!

I'll yell at you if I want to!

Why don't you keep them on your side of the room!

They are on my side!

I don't know what started the argument but I'd never seen them this angry at each other. During the last few years Joanie had changed from a happy little girl into a frustrated and combative teenager. But I didn't care. I just stayed out of it like I did all the other arguments in the family. I got something to eat and then went to the park. But their argument carried over into the next day.

Growing weary of the argument I grabbed my ball and glove and headed outside to throw the ball against the house. I saw Uncle Joe walking up the walkway.

Where's Shirley?

She's upstairs.

Not saying another word to me, he walked into house and yelled for Shirley to come downstairs.

What do you want, Uncle Joe?

We need to go to Grandma's house.

Why?

I'll tell you on the way there.

Shirley came down followed by Joanie. Both had scowls on their faces, arms folded, not speaking to each other.

Shirley immediately took the front seat, with Joanie and I in the back. As we drove off, Uncle Joe looked at Shirley and in a nonchalant manner said, Your papa. . . Nick is no longer with us.

What does that mean?

He died today.

He died? No! Why did it have to happen now? Tears coming down her face.

Shirley was dating Wendell and they were planning to get married. But Uncle Nick, wouldn't be walking her down the aisle, his little girl's arm entwined in his. The daddy who had his little girl sit on his lap, the little girl he used to take fishing. He wouldn't be giving his little girl away at her wedding because he died of massive heart attack at the age of 42.

Looking at each other, Joanie and I certainly didn't know what to say or how to comfort her, especially Joanie, her eyes down and looking guilty because she had been quarreling with Shirley.

At Grandma's house all the Aunts were crying. Aunt Jenny was hysterical. Aunt Margaret was explaining to Pop what happened when Uncle Nick came to Grandma's house that day.

He looked pale and asked if he could lie down on a bed. I told him to use Donnie's room. That was about ten. At noon I peeked into the room and he wasn't moving. He didn't look right. That's when I decided to wake him up, but he didn't budge, so I called the ambulance.

That night lying in bed I could hear Aunt Jenny in the kitchen in hysterics. Angry and bitter. How could God let this happen? Why is he doing this? What kind of a God is he? I don't want to be alive. There's nothing for me to live for.

Chapter 26

Because of the funeral I didn't get back to school until Thursday. Before school I walked across the playground and spotted the guys playing marbles. Since I thought I had been accepted, I approached them immediately.

Hi, guys, can I play?

No, said Mickey. We have someone else who's playing with us. I looked around but didn't see anyone. They kept their heads down and didn't say anything. I stayed there for a few moments feeling awkward and embarrassed then left quickly so I wouldn't make a fool of myself.

These guys think they're uppity up with their smug attitude. They think they're better than you because they're in regular class and you're not.

Walking into the building and up the stairs, I was brought out of my thoughts by Miss Towne.

Good morning, Jimmy. How are you this morning?

Okay, I guess. Shrugging my shoulders.

What's the matter?

Nothing.

Yes, there is. I can always tell when something is bothering you. Your head's down. Now what's the problem?

I told her what happened with the marble guys.

Well, Jimmy, you must realize that sometimes that will happen. There are some very cruel people in the world. Not everything is perfect in life. You're just going to have to make the best of it.

What if it was the other way around? If they were in special education and I was in a regular class and I treated them like that. How would they react?

I don't know, Jimmy. How would you treat them? Would you act just like them?

I never forgot what they did. It taught me a lesson. I was stupid for thinking that everything was honky dory and they would let me play with them. I should have known better. As long as I was in special education I would never ever be considered their equal or anyone's equal. I knew where I stood.

I pouted all the way home. Angry and hurt at what they did.

Rushing into the kitchen, I headed for the refrigerator and grabbed a piece of blueberry pie and headed outside.

How was school today, Jimmy?

Fine, Mom. I hurried out of the kitchen so I didn't have to talk to her. I headed for a walk in the vacant lot down the street.

I was there just a few minutes when I heard two sounds like a zap and immediately felt two stings. One on my side and the second on my upper leg. Looking up I saw them on the porch laughing at me at me, but I didn't see what was so funny. Angry and mad I yelled at them. Why did you do that? They were new to the country. Somewhere near a country called Russia.

You don't belong in this field! Yelling in broken English.

It's not your field! Yelling back at them, as one of the young boys came down to challenge me.

I was so mad for being BB shot that I was on top of him in a matter of seconds. I put the palm of my hand across his face and nose and pushed as hard as I could to hurt him. This was one time I had the advantage. His buddies sensed that I had the best of him and called him to back to the porch. I should've hit him harder and hurt him. Instead I got up and let him go and walked home.

When Mom saw me she went into a tirade, but I never told her what happened.

You've been fighting again, haven't you! What's the matter with you, Jimmy?

Leave him alone, Lena. I've told you before the boy needs to learn to fight his own battles. I'm not raising a sissy for a son.

Since Uncle Nick's death the house had been real quiet. I think everyone was still in shock from the quick way he died. Mom and Pop were even taking a break from yelling and fighting with each other.

Joanie was feeling sorry for arguing with Shirley, but since I didn't know what to say to either of them, I used the best diplomacy possible. Like I always did when confronted with a family predicament, I stayed out of it.

Chapter 27

Jimmy!

I didn't answer.

Jimmy! You need to come home! Dad wants to talk to us,

I didn't want to go home or be bothered by anybody. I preferred the peace and quiet of the park. But remembering the last time I didn't get home right away, I slouched behind her and headed back to the house.

We're moving, said Pop. To Shonnard Street.

Great! I said. And I meant it. I was happy about moving from Marcella Street. All I needed to do was find a spot on this house and write Jimmy Was Here. We moved from Marcella Street to Shonnard Street within a week. And my new house was right across the street from Seymour School. The end of the big walk. Oh happy day!

And some other good stuff was about to happen. "On my honor I will do my best, to do my duty, to God and my country and to obey the Scout Law." Troop 35, Tuesday nights.

Pop asked me at supper one night if I would like to join the Boy Scouts.

Why?

It might help you.

How might it help me?

You might learn self-discipline and to be more mature and make new friends.

I make new friends at school, dad. Besides I don't fit in with those kinds of guys.

They'll be nice boys, Jimmy. And you remember Mr. Mackey. He lives right behind Grandma Corso.

Why don't you think about it?

Two weeks later I was a Tenderfoot. The troop met at a local church, which was a ten-minute walk from the house. But even better was the three-minute walk to school, which made it especially nice for lunch. But I was still smarting from the rejection of the smug marble gang.

The first thing I had to learn for the scouts was the Scout Oath and then recite it in front of the Scoutmaster and the other new Tenderfoots. I studied it most nights, memorizing every word so I would make a good impression on the guys and the scoutmaster, Mr. Mackey.

Several weeks later when the night arrived Mr. Mackey lined us up in a straight line, took attendance and then asked who would like to recite the oath. I raised my hand first hoping I could get called on and get it over with. All the guys there knew I was in special education so I really wanted to make a good impression.

Okay, Jimmy. You had your hand up first, go ahead.

I stepped out in front of group, nervous and not sure I could do it. But it shouldn't be that hard. It's just a bunch of words. Slowly and carefully I recited each one until I had completed the oath.

Very good, Jimmy. He looked surprised that I could do it. What did he expect? What did any of them expect? That I wasn't supposed to learn it, or repeat it? Because I was in special education? Maybe no one, at home or school, with good reason, thought I was capable of memorizing dates and events or even reasoning out things. I guess I had more to prove than I realized.

After we repeated the scout oath, Mr. Mackey asked us if we would like to sign up for Camp Woodland for one or two weeks in July. This sounded great because I liked being outdoors. I had no idea what we could possibly do for two weeks but it sure would be worth giving it a try. All I had to do was convince Mom that it was safe for me to be there.

No! Why do you want to go there! It's not safe!

But it will be fun, Mom. You told me to join the scouts because there were lots of things to do.

I don't care! It's not safe!

For Pete's sake, Lena, It will be safe! They will have all kinds of adult supervision!

How do we know they'll be there all the time! We don't know anything about them!

Damn it, Lena! He'll be fine! They wouldn't let any of the boys go if they felt it wasn't safe!

The following week I signed up for my first trip to Camp Woodland. I only hoped I would like it.

But Mom still wasn't convinced.

It will be all right, Mom! Nothing's going to happen!

How do we know that?

You can't protect me forever!

I'm not trying to protect you! I just don't think it's safe! You haven't leaned anything about life! That's why you're in special education!

I was stunned by her remark. It really hurt. I know she regretted it, but it was too late. The damage was done.

I'll never forget that, Mom.

Mom was an overprotective mother. She went too far in trying to save us. She caused more problems than she solved. I couldn't wait until I get out of the house!

Several days later Joanie and I wanted to go swimming at the park. It was an overcast day, but fairly warm, so we asked her if we could go swimming.

No!

But why!

Because I said so!

Lots of kids are going!

I don't care about the other kids!

It's a nice warm day!

I said no swimming! You can get polio! This has been a bad year for it and lots of kids are getting it. You can get it from swimming. No swimming and that's final!

I was glad when camp day arrived. At least I could go swimming when I wanted to. I was excited, but then again not sure if I would like it.

Mom and Pop drove me to camp and stayed with me until I got settled into my tent. Coming over to greet us was Mr. Mackey. Before Jimmy can do anything, he needs to go down to the lake and get a buddy pass for swimming. There'll be a lifeguard there to help him out and explain what he needs to do.

You allow them to go swimming?

Yes, Mrs. Corso. That's part of our program. There won't be any problems. All our young scouts swim with a buddy.

Walking down to the lake, we introduced ourselves to the lifeguard.

Can you swim out to that ladder?

Pop, thinking that it was on the ladder on the other side of lake, answered for me.

No!

But the ladder was only about fifty yards from us. I didn't even get a chance to tell them I could do it before he gave me the buddy pass. I should have said something instead of being quiet. I knew I could swim that far, and I shouldn't have let Pop speak for me. But it showed me the confidence, or more correctly, the lack of confidence, he had in me.

Finally they left. As they drove off I felt excited and happy for the first time in my life to be doing something different and unusual. I explored the area. I took a walk by the lake. It was different from the city. No cars or beeping horns and no large buildings, just peace and quiet among the large trees. It was beautiful. I loved the lake and the different kinds of trees and the smell of the forest. I didn't need to find a place to escape. I was already in it. A whole week of peace and quiet. No fighting. No hollering. No yelling. And none of Mom's, Because I said so!

I was assigned to a tent with a kid named Hutchinson, but we never became friends. I enjoyed all the activities of canoeing, first aid and safety, hiking on the trails with nature discussions, learning how to tie knots, and swimming in the cold lake. I even liked crafts, even though I was never very good at doing things with my hands.

The second day of camp the assistant to Mr. Mackey approached me asking me for a favor.

Yeh. Sure. Eager to please him. What can I get you?

I need a left-handed monkey wrench.

A what?

A left-handed monkey wrench.

Where do I get one?

One of the other campsites should have one.

I dashed off to the first campsite thinking they should have it.

Hi sir, I'm with troop 35. Do you have a left-handed monkey wrench we can borrow?

He looked at me with a sly smile on his face. No we don't, son. You'll need to go to the next campsite.

I dashed off again to the next campsite. Asking the same question and getting the same sly smile and answer.

Again I was off and running. Only this time I wasn't running fast. This time I was headed to a large tent. There were several scoutmasters sitting at a table drinking coffee. I asked them the same question and got the same smile.

How many campsites have you been to, son?

A few.

I think you've had enough, son. There is no such thing as a left-handed monkey wrench. It's an old prank that older boys play on first timers at camp.

When I got back to my campsite several of the boys and Mr. Mackey were laughing at me. I just laughed it off, showing them I could be a good sport. At least they weren't laughing at me because I was in special education.

Except for the monkey wrench incident, the rest of the week was great. I liked it so much I was able to convince Mom and Pop to let me stay another week.

———————————————————

Chapter 28

Fall 1952. The start of another school year. I didn't know how long we would be living on Shonnard Street across from Seymour School, but I did make a friend in Billy Brooks. He delivered newspapers and lived down the street with his folks and four sisters.

Saturdays we usually played football with his friends in another neighborhood. I enjoyed playing football, except, small as I was, I always was used as the center. The other boys wanted to be heroes by playing quarterback or catching the ball, especially when the girls were walking by and watching us. Yes, we now noticed the girls who once had "cooties," but now had curves that definitely got our attention.

After the game Billy, as usual, gave me a ride home on his bike.

On the way back he invited me to his house for Kool-Aid. When we walked into the kitchen his folks were laughing and seemed to be enjoying themselves. As I got to know them I was impressed by the way the family treated each other. They seemed to personify the typical family of the times, treating each other with respect. They were well organized and seemed to have a well functioning family. I never heard his folks yell or swear at each other.

At supper that night I asked Pop if I could have a bike. It was like getting blood from a rock.

Why do you need a bike? I never had one. You can walk to school, to Boy Scouts and to your friend's house. He can take you anywhere.

That's just it dad. I have to ride on his crossbars everywhere we go. I need my own bike.

We'll see. Right now I want to watch "Life with Luigi." It's about this Italian guy that owns an antique shop.

After fifteen minutes he got up and left.

I don't like this program. If they don't show us in the Mafia then they show us as too fun loving and not very smart.

A week later I had a bike with a basket on the front handlebars. It was an old bike, but it moved, and that's what was important.

Saturday we played football and it felt good riding my own bike. On the way back Billy asked me if I saw the movie "Bwana Devil."

No. Is it good?

It's in 3-D. You can watch it with special cardboard glasses.

How does that work? Just then the chain came off my bike forcing us to walk home.

You better have your dad help you put that chain back on. And make sure it's tight.

That night at dinner I told Pop my chain fell of my bike. I need your help to put it back on the bike.

We'll see. I'm busy tomorrow.

A week went by before he helped me.

I'll help you now, but if it breaks again you'll have to fix it yourself.

Billy said to make sure it's on tight.

Then have Billy fix it next time.

Several days later it broke again.

Pop, the chain broke again.

What did I tell you the last time I fixed it? I don't have time to keep fixing it. You'll just have to walk.

As for school, it was the same thing as last year. Miss Towne still worked with us on life skills. That was something that never changed and the class work was the same. Everything was the same except that Chucky was gone. I never asked Miss Towne what happened to him, nor did I care.

Christmas was getting near, so for crafts I made Mom two dishes as a gift. One was of our new dog Pinky and the other was a nativity scene.

Through all the years, all the moves, Mom's breakdowns, her cancer and the fire, she saved those dishes. They now hang on my bookshelf.

With the winter months came my annual bout of bronchitis and a visit by Dr.Grant to give me my penicillin shot.

Thank God for Fleming!

Who?

Alexander Fleming. He discovered penicillin. Haven't you learned about him in school?

No.

What about Galileo, Newton, Pasteur and the Curies?

No. We have lots of slow kids in my class. Most can barely read. Miss Towne does the best she can. We do lots of life skill activities and some current events. We don't do arithmetic, English, social studies or science.

Chapter 29

The school year finally ended and the first day of summer vacation was here. As usual, I got up earlier than Joanie. Walking into the kitchen, Mom and Pop were talking. Pop never minced any words.

Jimmy, were moving.

What do you mean?

That's just what I mean. Shirley and Wendel are getting married. Aunt Jenny is going to live with grandma until they come back from their honeymoon then she is going to live with them.

What's that got to do with us?

I can't afford to pay the rent on this house, so we need to move.

Where to?

Aunt Connie's

What school will I be going to?

Seymour.

How will I get here?

You'll take the bus. You'll need to get up early and transfer to the bus that takes you to Seymour.

I was disgusted. Is there anything else you need to tell me?

Yes. You're going to have to sleep on a cot in the dining room. Aunt Connie has rented out the spare room to earn some extra money.

Two days later we drove out of the driveway passing the pile of trash on the curb with my bike on top. I never got another bike, and I don't know what ever happened to Billy.

Chapter 30

This was a nice house with four pear trees on one side of the house. I loved eating those pears, but I hated sleeping in the dining room. It was the pathway to the kitchen. Everyone was always passing my cot. Day and night. I hated it. I wanted my own room. A boy going through puberty needs his own room.

The only saving grace was that I met a kid named Tony at the local hangout store on the corner of Teal Street. He and some of his friends loved to play baseball in a field right down the street from the house.

You should try out for baseball, Jimmy.

Nah. I don't think I could make the team. My arm is not very good.

You can hit the ball.

But not very far.

You can hit singles, plus you can play second base. That would be a good place for you.

A week later I was at the early morning tryouts for the team. The coach never said if I was good or bad. He just said he would call us in a few days.

At supper that night I made sure everyone at the house knew I was getting a call.

Coach Tony is going to call me in a few days to tell me if I made the team. I've never tried out for anything before. I'm okay at fielding, and I can hit the ball but not far. I just have to wait and see what he thinks.

The call came the next day.

Hi, Jimmy. This is coach Tony.

Yeh, I'm sorry but…blah, blah, blah. I hung up the phone and headed to the back yard.

Was that the coach, Jimmy?

Yeh, Joanie. He said I had lots of hustle. That I tried real hard and he wished the other boys would try as hard as me, but I don't have a good enough arm and can't hit the ball very far. I grabbed my ball and glove as I headed to the back yard, crying and angry. I wanted to make this team. I needed to make this team.

Life is sure weird. The following week I got another call from coach Tony.

Hi, Jimmy, this is coach.

Yeh?

How would you like to be back on the team?

Sure. But why?

Jimmy, you try real hard in practice. Harder than most of the other guys. And I need a backup at second base. You can really help the team.

The backup at second base turned into a starting position for me. Not only that, but I even was the hero for one game when I hit a bloop single over third base, driving in the winning run.

Chapter 31

But too soon, like all great summer vacations, the season changed into September, the start of yet another school year. Getting up early and walking to the bus stop. Waiting for the bus. Transferring to another bus. This was not my idea of a good time. Instead of walking across the street to school, I now had to travel across the city. Instead of a five-minute walk, I now had a sixty-minute bus ride. What a waste of time. Add to this, the fact I'm still in special education and I sleep on a cot in the dining room. No wonder I was grouchy and moody. And to top it all off I had two new enemies. Eddie and Charles.

I wanted off the bus and out of Seymour School. I put the subject up for discussion at dinner that night.

I'd sure like to be in regular class instead of this special education class.

Be happy where you are. The class is good for you. That was Mom's response.

Pop's surprising response as he put down his wine glass was, Why don't you ask Miss Towne tomorrow and see what she says?

The next day when I asked Miss Towne about the possibility of trying regular class, her response was, Why?

Because I think I can do it. You have to admit my reading has improved. I'm above the kids in this class and I know my understanding of what I read is really better than them.

What do your parents think of this idea?

Mom's against it, Pop's for it.

Jimmy, there are a lot of reasons why you are in special education. It's just not reading. It's other skills like self-discipline and paying attention and adjusting to other people. You didn't make any effort in regular class before you came here. Why the interest now about getting in a regular class?

Because I think I can do it. Besides, don't you see any progress in my reading?

Yes, I do. But like I just said there are lots of other things to consider.

What's wrong with giving me a chance? Can there be any harm? I've been in special education since I was nine. I think I deserve a chance.

I'll see what I can do. I will talk to Mrs. Dunham in social studies and see if she would be willing to take you for two weeks for her next unit. That's the best I can do.

Thank you. I'll tell my mom and dad what's happening.

What I didn't realize was that Eddie and Charles overheard some of the conversation. As I walked back to my desk they were laughing at me.

Hey, Corso, what are you going into regular class for? You don't belong with them.

I didn't say anything to them. They were just like Chucky, but I knew I could hold my own against them if I got into a fight.

Two weeks later I was in Mrs. Dunham's social studies class. I took the last seat in the third row, right in the middle of the classroom. This enabled me to see the blackboard and any notes she wrote on the board.

When I headed to my seat the kids looked at me, but didn't say anything. Although most of them didn't know my name I knew they recognized me as being from the special education room.

Every day I took notes faithfully. I put down every word verbatim. Even If I thought it wasn't important, I wrote down the word or phrase or whatever she was discussing.

After social studies class I went back to the special education room for the rest of the day. There to feel the wrath of Eddie.

Why are you in regular class! You don't belong in there!

It's none of your business.

You're a dummy, just like the rest of us!

And so it went for the next two weeks. For some unknown reason my situation bothered Eddie and Charles. They never let up, constantly challenging me about trying to be in a regular class.

It all came to head one day while I was waiting for the bus to go home. They lived in the area and were riding their bikes when they saw me standing at the bus stop. They came over and started the same taunting they did in the classroom. Eddie got off his bike and came right at me, laughing and saying the same old thing, Why are you in regular class? You don't belong in no regular class. He shoved me. I don't think I even blinked. I was on top of him in seconds.

I told you, it's none of your business!

He tried to get up, but I had him pinned to the ground. I was sitting on top of him, and I punched him, hard, in the mouth. Then I held his arms down and yelled at him. It's none of your damn business! He realized I was stronger than him and went limp. I hated him. I wanted to really hurt him. Then I saw the bus coming, so I got off him. But he wasn't laughing and neither was Charlie. I never had any problems with them the rest of the school year.

My two weeks were over. The last day of the unit Mrs. Dunham gave us a 100-point test. I had studied hard for the test. Memorizing every word on my notes. Mom and Pop never offered to help me study.

When test day arrived I was nervous. I wanted to get started right away because I was afraid I might forget some important information. I quickly scanned the test, and it seemed like I knew most of the information. I answered every question, turned in my paper, and then waited the long weekend to get my test back on Monday.

Sitting in the special education room, I couldn't wait until the bell rang for third period social studies. Hurrying down the hall and into the room, I made eye contact with Mrs. Dunham, but she didn't smile or make any comment. Taking my seat I studied the faces of some of the other kids. One boy was staring out the window like he didn't care. Another boy had his head on his desk and seemed bored with everything.

Finally after attendance she handed out the papers. When she came to me she smiled, and gave me my paper. 78%. 78%!

I was ecstatic. I wanted to stand up and shout, See my paper! I can do this! After class I hurried back to show Miss Towne my paper.

Very good, Jimmy!

I was proud. Even Mom and Pop were happy. Now that I showed them I could do well on a test, they would have to let me into a regular classroom. And that's the idea the three of us presented to Miss Towne the next morning.

It's not that easy. Just because Jimmy scored well on this one test doesn't mean he can go into the mainstream program.

Why not?

Because there a lot of other factors to consider.

Like what?

When Jimmy came into this class it wasn't just because of his academics. There were also emotional and discipline problems. Remember he scored a 70 on his I.Q. test. He couldn't concentrate on his work and his reading was very poor.

But he's made progress.

Yes, he has, Mr. Corso, but it's not that easy to let him out of special education.

Why not?

Once students are placed into this program they must stay for a minimum of three years.

Three years! Pop and I said together.

Why weren't we told this before he came here?

I assumed everybody knew the district policy.

So that means I'm stuck?

I'm sorry, but that's the way it is.

What about staying in Mrs. Dunham's class the rest of the semester?

She has to follow the policy. There's nothing she can do no matter how well you scored on the test. There's nothing we can do until next year.

At lunchtime I sat in the courtyard thinking and pouting about my predicament.

Hey, what did you score on that test? It was one of the boys from my social studies class.

78%. What did you get?

F. I hate school. I can't wait until I'm sixteen so I can quit.

What irony. Here I'm trying to get into the regular class, and he gets an F and wants to quit school. I wonder how many kids did worse than me and yet can stay in the regular class? And yet, I can understand him hating school and wanting to quit. I know how he feels. Even though I scored well on my test, I still had definite feelings about wanting to quit school, and yet I wanted to prove I could pass regular classes. But I decided if the committee wouldn't let me into regular classes, I might just as well quit school and join the service.

The only good thing in my life was that I finally got my own room where I could turn up the radio and hear the powerful voice of Al Martino sing "Here in my Hear" and listen to baseball and basketball games.

———————————

Chapter 32

The other good thing was the school year was over, and that meant the first week of baseball. I made the team again and played second base. I was a little chatterbox, always yelling at the opposing batter. Hey, battah, battah! I guess it was my way of showing the guys that I really wanted to be part of the team.

After the games we always walked home. On one of these walks one of the guys started talking about a dad that was touching one of the girls he knew.

Being naive I asked him what he meant.

Haven't you heard of incest?

No. I was embarrassed that I didn't know what they meant.

It's when a father touches or has sex with his daughter. Sometimes Uncles do the same thing.

I felt frozen. I felt sick. I could barely hear him talking. Incest. The word kept going through my mind. It all made sense now. Her attitude. Sarcastic and snotty. Arguing and defensive. And now she'd started smoking. That's why she never wanted to go to picnics or to the park or even be around him. Who could blame her for not wanting to be around him? Was there any justice for this little girl, my own sister? Why wasn't God there to protect her? Or was it God's will? I thought cynically.

The "good" Catholic men in the family once went to church every Sunday and even received Communion. But for some reason they stopped going.

I don't get anything out of it, was their favorite answer.

I was confused because I thought we went to church to worship and pray to God. It's what you give, not receive. They should be happy.

They've been living the American Dream. Good jobs, good pay and they even owned their own homes.

Oh, yeh, that's right, except for us. We kept moving and always rented or leased, then moved. And that's what happened that summer. Right in the middle of my baseball season. We were gone. Again.

There was no sense in arguing. It was always Pop's way. We never had any say about what was happening.

Making an adjustment in the middle of the summer wasn't easy. And Pop wouldn't even take me to Aunt Connie's so I could still play baseball.

You and Joanie can make new friends here. There are plenty of kids your own age in this neighborhood. As for baseball, you can join a team around here.

Joanie also had a hard time adjusting to the many moves. And the other thing must have been getting to Joanie because she and Mom had a bad argument about going somewhere.

I said no! You can't go!

But I have a chance to meet some new friends. I want to go to this party.

I said no!

But why?

Because I said so! Now go to your room!

Later that evening Mom decided she better check on Joanie. Moments later she came running out of her room.

Jim she's gone again! She went out the window. And the bedroom smells like smoke.

It didn't take Mom and Pop long to figure where she went. They found her at the party. It was the third time she had run away from home.

Chapter 33

Fall of 1954. Joanie and I are at Grant School. I was in some kind of special class, but it was nothing like Seymour school. The last week of October the school transferred me to another special education class at Franklin School taught by Mrs. Rhiner whose style was much different than Miss Towne's. We had assigned seats, and mostly because we were now older, the noise level was quieter than in Miss Towne's class. Just like Seymour School, I was always glad when the bell rang at the end of the day. I had almost made it to the door when Mrs. Rhiner called me to her desk.

Yeh?

Jimmy I received your transcript. Your files show you've been in special education for some time. But I also called Miss Towne at Seymour. She told me about your two weeks in social studies class. Just before you left she did go to the committee, but she never saw or heard from you again.

Yeh. We move a lot.

Miss Towne told me the committee rejected your request to enter regular class. They felt that just because you scored well on one test didn't mean you would be successful in all your classes. There are too many other blah, blah, blah.

But I've been trying. I know I have a long way to go. I deserve a chance. What about when my three years are up? Can I be evaluated again?

No. You've been evaluated. You're in special education permanently. I'm sorry there's nothing that can be done.

That's not fair.

Sometimes life works that way, Jimmy. It can be tough, even cruel.

Mrs. Rhiner seemed sad, but she was right, life can be cruel. Especially for her. A year later, and only in her thirties, she died of cancer.

More and more I could understand Joanie's bad attitude. I was frustrated and tired of moving. I decided to talk to Mom to see if she would say something to Pop. After school seemed to be the best time because Pop was usually working, but when I walked into the parlor Mom was sitting on Pop's lap crying. She seemed confused and didn't seem to know what was happening.

What's wrong with Mom?

Nothing. Just go outside and play and I'll tell you later.

Later never came. We moved. Again. On a cold, snowy day in late February 1955, right in the middle of the school year, we arrived in Oswego.

What kind of business does Uncle Gus have?

Windows, Joanie. We're going to put in windows.

We're too far from home, Jim. I want to be closer to Ma and Pa.

Lena, we've discussed this before. It's only a thirty-minute drive to Syracuse.

It's still too far.

I was quiet on the trip. Angry and quiet. Mostly angry. But I kept thinking about my dream. It was a simple stupid little dream. I'm outside on a cloudy day, laying on my back and looking at the clouds. Suddenly a cloud stops right over me at takes the shape of a gray duck with an orange beak and feet. The duck flies down to a muddy spot and rolls some mud between his feet into a ball and jumps in front of me. He kicks the ball on top of the water then flies away. A man and woman are standing next to the stream. The man says to the woman, don't tell me that ducks are dumb. They're smart.

Chapter 34

Oswego was okay. It was a nice community, but as always, we never bought a house. We rented a house on Third Street and then I enrolled in special education in Oswego High School, my ninth school. I was fourteen years old, and it was looking more and more like the service for me.

Because of my age I was allowed to take a physical education and a music class. This helped to break up the monotony of being in the same class all day. But I was still smarting from being rejected by the committee and permanently relegated to special education.

I needed physical activity. On a snowy, blustery afternoon, on the way to the drug store for Mom, I saw some guys going into the Y. It would be great if I could join, giving me something to do after school. My biggest problem would be to convince Pop. Of course, the first thing he would ask was the cost, so I stopped in on my way home. It was twenty-five cents. Much to my surprise Pop said I could join, so after supper I put on my rubber boosts, bundled up, braved the cold weather and headed to the Y. I gave my quarter to the man who gave me a punch card.

You new in town?

Yeh, we just arrived a few days ago.

Play any sports?

No.

What grade you in?

Special education.

What kind of a class is that?

For kids who don't do well in regular class. Things like that.

Why don't you do well?

I don't know. I guess I don't care.

You don't have much pride in yourself, do you?

What's that?

How you feel about yourself. Your work. How you do things.

I didn't give his words much thought but the remark did stay in the back of my mind.

Hey, can I go swimming?

Yeh. But make sure you shower first. Naked. He laughed.

Naked! I didn't know if he was kidding or not, but I did bring my bathing suit with me. I walked into the locker room but I was reluctant to take off my clothes for fear of embarrassing myself. I had hair between my legs and I thought that wasn't normal. I kept thinking I might have some disease. I was afraid to even ask anyone about it. I watched some older men go into the locker room but I hung back so they wouldn't see me. When the coast was clear I hurried and undressed and took a quick shower. But I couldn't get out fast enough. Another man came into the shower but I noticed he also had hair between his legs. Did we both have a disease? I can laugh about it now, but I had no idea what was happening to my body. I was confused about puberty and the sudden emergence of hair where once I was bald.

I enjoyed the Y. I went as much as I could during the week, plus weekends. I played lots of basketball but was always the last one chosen in pick-up games.

The cold winter turned into spring and Mother's Day. Mom and Pop went to early mass by themselves. Wanting to do something nice for her, I set the table and made breakfast. But they never came home until afternoon. True to his character, Pop took Mom out to breakfast but never considered taking Joanie and I so we could be together as a family. When they got home Mom saw the table and the cold cooked breakfast.

That was very nice of you, Jimmy. She seemed almost ashamed of what they had done. She knew I felt hurt. Pop never said a word.

Things weren't going very well with Pop and the window business. To make matters worse, Mom took our dog Pinky out for an afternoon walk. I was home for lunch, sitting at the table when I heard the screeching of wheels and brakes and then Mom's scream. Pinky got caught under the back wheels of the truck. Pop and I rushed downstairs and saw Mom crying and holding Pinky in her arms. We rushed her to the vet, but she died in Mom's arms on the way there. Mom never got over the loss of that dog, even though just a few weeks later she got another dog. He was a hyper, sensitive, and neurotic cocker spaniel who she named Buffy.

Several weeks later we, of course, moved to another part of Oswego. There I headed to the local hangout to get a soda and a guy names Ross started up a conversation with me.

You new around here?

Yeh. Jimmy Corso. We came here a few weeks ago from Syracuse. I lived close to the Y, then my dad found this house down the street.

What grade you in?

God, I always hated when someone asked me that question. Embarrassment. Shame. I sputtered a few words, then sheepishly said, Special education.

My sister's in special education! I'm not sure why but we both acted surprised.

What's your sister's name?

Margi.

Just then one of his friends came over and joined us.

This is Jimmy Corso. He's new in town. He's in my sister's class.

The one for the retards?

I glared at him, but true to my nature didn't say anything to defend myself or the kids in my class. Ross could see I was upset with his remark. But unlike me, he was not afraid to speak up and defend his sister's class.

They're not like that Sammy! You know Margi's in that class! And you know better than to talk like that!

I felt ashamed and should have defended myself instead of letting someone else do it for me.

As the weeks progressed into summer I hooked up with Tommy Jumbo, another friend of Ross', and with several more of guys from his class. We wound up playing lots of baseball. One day we had about twelve guys playing when a guy wearing a white tee shirt that said East Side Recreation Center interrupted our game.

Hi guys, how ya doing?

Fine, we mumbled, curious about why he was interrupting our game.

I'm in charge of the Rec Center for activities. Do you guys like to run?

We shrugged our shoulders, looking at each other, wondering what he wanted.

The district wants to have a race between the east and west sides of town. Are any of you guys interested?

What do we have do?

You have to race against each other. The winner of you guys will race next week in the hundred-yard dash against the top guy from the east side. Is anyone interested?

There were a few moments of silence as we all looked at each other.

I am, said Tommy.

Me too, said Ross.

Okay, follow me.

Me too, I heard myself say.

We all followed him to the middle of a large field.

Okay, I want all of you to line up on this spot. I'm going down the field about eighty yards. When I blow my whistle I want you guys to run as hard as you can to me. The guy who wins runs next week.

The whistle blew and we were off. I was in the middle of the pack about half way into the race not far from the lead guys. But I was speeding up. I was in fourth, then third, then second. To my surprise I won. I was happy but oddly calm as he called me over to him.

What's your name?

Jimmy Corso

Okay, Jimmy Corso. Next Friday you be at the west side park at six in the evening. You'll race the 100-yard dash against the winner of the east side of town.

When I got home I excitedly told Pop about my race.

Guess what?

What?

When I was playing baseball this afternoon this guy from the east side rec center came over and asked us to race. And I won.

That's good.

But that's not all. Because I won, I get to race the top kid in my age group next week at their park. It's next Friday at six. Can you come?

We'll see. Right now I have other things on my mind.

That was it. I went to the race by myself. I watched the older boys race. It was a long time before they got to my division of thirteen and fourteen year olds. When the time finally came, it was nearly dark. The guy next to me was a little taller and he wore some kind of special shoes to help him run better. He dug two holes, one for each foot and got down in the starting position. I just stood up. I didn't know any better. The whistle blew and we were off. Again I was in the middle of the group, and like before, I was gaining speed. As we approached the finish line I pulled even with the leader and lunged forward. I thought I had won, but they said we tied. We flipped for the first place medal. I lost and took home the second. I was upset because I thought I won, but I was also happy because for the first time in my life I had won something

But really, nothing in my life changed much. In the fall of 1955, Joanie entered tenth grade, and I was in my sixth year of special education classes. Except for the glee club and gym class, everything was the same. Same classroom. Same teacher. The only thing I enjoyed was going to the Y. One Saturday morning while waiting in the small entrance for the Y to open, I was standing with several older boys that I played with in pick-up basketball games. This one guy named Smitty was in his late twenties. I never liked him and I think he knew it.

Hey, Corso, have you ever felt another man's penis?

The other guys laughed but they seemed embarrassed.

No! I said with a disgusted tone in my voice.

Well, here. You can feel mine.

Before I could say anything he had it out and pushed it across my face. I pushed him off me, but he was much bigger and stronger.

You're a jerk! Get outta here!

Nobody calls me a jerk, you little shit!

He was ready to do it again and started to come towards me.

That's enough, Smitty! It was one of his friends. When the jerk realized the other guys didn't think it was funny, he backed off.

I was just fooling around. He laughed.

I got over it, but I never forgot it.

Chapter 35

During football season Ross, Tommy and the rest of us would go to the big varsity football game on Saturday afternoons. After the games we always played touch football, which ended up being more like tackle. On one particular Saturday afternoon, a group of girls was watching us. Of course, all the guys were showing off, throwing or catching the ball and running for a touchdown.

We ended our game early because the girls came over to talk us. The Sadie Hawkins dance was a few weeks away and I think some of the girls wanted to ask some of us to go. I recognized one of the girls from lunchtime when she and her friends sat on the long wall outside the baseball field watching us play softball. To my surprise she came over to talk to me. I didn't know what to say, and the less I said the better off I was. The rest of the guys were acting kind of stupid and goofy while the girls seemed very mature. After a short time they left and us guys walked home.

Puberty and hormones were taking over our bodies. Girls made us act and think stupid. The rest of the guys started to talk about which girl they hoped would ask them to the dance. I didn't say anything because I knew no girl was interested in me. At least I thought no girl was interested in me.

Hey, Corso, what do you think of Sandy?

I think she's nice. Why?

She kinda likes you.

I was surprised. I knew once, when we were living with Aunt Connie, that Susie Morola had liked me, but then I was more interested in playing baseball than in girls. But now hormones were shooting through my body and I was well aware of girls.

So what does that mean?

It means she might ask you to the Sadie Hawkins dance. She's in my biology class. I'm pretty sure she would go out with you.

I don't think so. I'm in special education. You guys know that.

Ross and I are going to ask her friends to the movies next week. Would you like to ask her and we'll all go together?

I guess.

I've been over to her house. Why don't I tell her we'll come see her Saturday? That way it will give you a chance to get to know each other.

Okay.

So on Saturday morning Tom, Ross and I hitchhiked to her house. She lived in Baldswinville about half way between Oswego and Syracuse. When we got to her house I was amazed at how big it was. Her mom met us at the door and showed us to the den.

Wow! Look at this den, Ross.

It's that expensive knotty pine stuff.

And look at that fireplace! And those hunting trophies?

Yeh. Her dad must be a hunter.

I think you're right, Ross. Look at all those stuffed heads of deer and elk. This den is longer than my house. In fact, this house is bigger than anything I have ever been in.

Yea. Me too, Corso.

There was a long moment of silence.

I'm out of my league.

What's that mean?

It's that old saying--she's a Cadillac. I'm a Chevy.

Give yourself a chance, Corso.

Does she know I'm in special ed?

What difference does that make?

A lot. Shhh. Here she comes with her folks. Don't say anything about me being in special education.

After a brief introduction we all sat down to talk.

Play any sports, Jimmy?

No. Just some basketball at the Y. We moved here from Syracuse in the middle of the school year.

That must be hard for you in school. What grade you in?

There was that damn question again. I hated it, but I had to answer him. I'm in special education, sir.

Oh? He stared at Sandy. I could read his mind. What is she thinking about, liking this guy?

Well, if you kids will excuse me, I've got some work to do.

After he left, we went out on her back porch and talked. Sandy and I actually hit it off great. We all agreed to go to the movies next Saturday and I told Sandy I would call her in a few days. We headed home.

I think you're in, Corso.

Really?

You can tell just by the way she acts towards you.

We'll see. I was always a pessimist. I'm going to call her in a few days. What time are we going to meet the girls next Saturday?

Ross and I think about 7. Sandy's Mom will drop off the girls in front of the theater.

I called her up on Tuesday. I was real nervous. I had never talked on the phone with a girl before. We did the usual small talk about her teachers. Who she liked and didn't like. Who was funny. Who cared or didn't care.

So, I guess we are all set for Saturday night?

No. I'm sorry, Jimmy, but I can't make it Saturday.

I thought everything was set with all of us?

Some things have changed, and I can't make it.

Well…Okay. I guess I'll see you later. I hung up the phone not wanting to prolong my embarrassment. I had that sick, empty feeling in my stomach. Angry at my rejection, I immediately called Tom.

I thought you said everything was set for Sandy and me on Saturday?

It was. What happened?

She said she couldn't make it.

I don't understand. I'll give her a call and then call you right back.

I waited anxiously until he called.

So what happened?

Her parents said you are a nice boy, but that you are in special education, and they want her to ask another boy to the Sadie Hawkins dance.

I was stunned and didn't say anything for a few moments.

I thought you said that wasn't a problem!

Sandy said it wasn't for her, but her parents had a real concern about her going anywhere with you. It had to do about how her parents' friends would see it.

You've got to be kidding! It's only a date to the movies and maybe the dance.

I guess it's a social thing, Corso.

What do I have to do? Show them the medal I won?

I don't think it would make any difference, Corso. Some people are just like that. Her family has lots of money and are real concerned about social stuff.

I don't understand why it's such a big deal.

Why don't you ask someone else?

Are you kidding? It would be the same thing.

You don't know that. Why don't you give it a try?

I'm not going to embarrass myself again. Is this the way it's always going to be with girls?

I didn't see Sandy during lunch for several weeks. Then the day before the dance I was outside during the lunch playing softball when I saw her sitting on the wall holding hands with some guy.

On the night of the dance I went to the local hangout and played pinball. Tom and Ross came by with their dates. We made some idle talk then they headed out to the dance. I watched as they walked up the street holding hands with their girls.

Months later I was still angry and hurt about my rejection. And, as a matter of fact, on March 1st 1956, I made a vow never to tell another girl, or her family, that I was in special education. And I never did.

Chapter 36

We moved again. In the middle of the school, again. Again I never said good-bye to anyone. This time we were staying with Mom's brother, Uncle Ernie and his wife Florence in Saranac Lake.

My first day there I was up early. I walked into the kitchen and saw Mom sitting at the table drinking her tea.

Why did we come here, Mom?

She just sounded disgusted. Pop was having problems in the window business so he and Uncle Gus decided to sell it.

But couldn't he find another job in Oswego? Or even Syracuse?

I don't know, Jimmy. You know how your dad is. If things don't go right he just moves to another place. I even got a letter from Aunt Mickey accusing me of ruining the business. She thinks I was the one who made it fail.

You? I was laughing. You don't know anything about the business. How could it be your fault? And why did we come here? This little rinky-dink place! There's nothing here! Aunt Florence said only six thousand people live here and they mostly rely on tourists. What kind of a job can he find here?

Only God knows, Jimmy!

And what kind of kids live in this hick town?

Dad's going to go with you and Joanie to school. I don't want to go outside in this blizzard.

I laughed cynically. It's warm today! It's only zero. Two weeks ago it got down to forty below.

Chapter 37

So Pop took us to school. Saranac Lake High School, my tenth school, and our third school this year.

Pop talked to the secretary. She briefly left the room then came back with Mr. St. Hill, a gray-haired gentleman, who wore glasses and was only slightly taller than Pop. They had a brief conversation. Pop filled out a card then handed it to him.

You're from Oswego?

Yes, but originally from Syracuse.

That's a very big school system compared to us. We have a K-12 school. Our senior class has ninety students, if that. Your card says Joanie is in tenth grade, but you haven't given me any information on Jimmy.

I need to talk to you about Jimmy.

Okay. Let me take Joanie upstairs to our senior high principal, Mr. Murphy, so he can get her started in classes.

A few minutes later Mr. St. Hill was back talking to Pop and me. Well, mainly to Pop, of course.

Now, Mr. Corso, what about Jimmy?

But I was only half listening. My thoughts were back in Oswego and being rejected by Sandy and her parents.

Jimmy's special education.

How long has he been in special education?

Since he was nine.

Mr. St. Hill looked at the card, then at Pop, then at me.

It says he's fifteen. In fact he's almost fifteen and a half.

Yes.

Is Joanie his older sister?

No, they're twins.

133

My thoughts drifted back to Oswego, not hearing what they were saying. After a few moments Mr. St. Hill left the room.

What's going on, dad?

I'll tell you later.

A few minutes later Mr. St. Hill came back with a tall man named Mr. Young.

After clearing his throat, Mr. St Hill said, Currently special education for Jimmy isn't an option here at Saranac Lake. So because of his background we feel it's best that he be placed in the seventh grade. At fifteen and half, he's almost too old for seventh grade, but he doesn't have any foundation for eighth grade. And seventh grade won't be easy. He's going from six years of special education into a seventh grade class that has many outstanding students. Later, if he's successful, he will go into the non-regents, or the non-college bound, high school program. If he doesn't do well the rest of this year, we will have to take him out of regular class and see where else we can put him.

My heart sank. I got that sick feeling. I just have to make it.

Chapter 38

Five minutes later I was walking down the hall with Mr. St. Hill and into the math class of Mrs. McKillip where she directed me to the last seat in the first row. The room was so quiet that I felt really uncomfortable. Even with my head down, I could still feel all the eyes of the kids looking at me.

As I sat down, I thought back to that one stupid test I took that sentenced me to special education. I thought about the committee that wouldn't reconsider my placement. Echoing also were the comments about my special education class at Seymour School, and the comments by all the other students at all the other schools I'd attended. And now here I sat, I'm not sure how or why, in a regular class. I'm wondering, will I be the class dummy, the slow learner, the retard I have been taught to believe I am? How will these kids react to me knowing I've been in special education for six years? I just won't let them know. This will be my new beginning. My new start. And I'm especially wondering if this chance is God's will. But then, there's also Pop's will. Will we move again?

Mrs. McKillip's voice intruded on my thoughts. I didn't know what she was talking about. Fractions? Adding, multiplying and subtracting fractions? I was horrified. Fractions?

When the bell rang I stepped into the crowded hallway and fumbled my way to Mrs. Alliason's English class. Again I was assigned to the last row, and again I had no idea what she was discussing. Prepositions. I had heard the word before but I didn't know how or why they were used. Maybe the next class would be easier to understand.

It was Citizenship Education taught by Mr. LaGoy. At least I know I am a citizen. I automatically sat down in the back row. The kids drifted into the room and took their seats. When the bell rang they stopped talking and took out their notebooks. All of them, except for two boys who didn't do anything. They didn't seem to care. They didn't take any notes and just doodled on their papers. I couldn't understand how they could be in a regular class and not take notes. Didn't they care?

Next was Mr. LeRoy's shop class. Shop wasn't new to me. Then Mr. Dorsch's Preliminary Science class. I had absolutely no idea about science, preliminary or otherwise, so, except for shop and gym, my other classes might just as well have been foreign languages.

My last class was something called Study Hall in room 210. The room looked like two classrooms put together. I handed my papers to a Miss Baker. She was a short, heavy- set lady with short wavy hair and glasses. She seemed nervous and fidgety as she assigned me to the back of the room. Taking my seat, I asked the boy next to me what kind of class this was.

It's just Study Hall. I haven't seen you around here. Didn't they have Study Hall where you came from?

No.

I didn't say anything else and just watched the kids as they came into the room. The bell rang. Some kids were late and no one was quiet even after she asked them repeatedly to settle down. I could see why she seemed nervous. This was the noisiest class I had been in all day, and it was obvious she didn't have any control over the situation. When the bell finally rang, I headed out the door.

Hey, where're you going? asked the kid next to me.

I'm headed home. Where're you going?

To the theater. My dad works there. He's also the mayor. My name's Bailey Anderson.

I'm Jimmy Corso. See ya later. As I left I looked back at him, not realizing we would form a friendship that would last 46 years until his untimely death of a massive heart attack at age 58.

I headed out the front door and down Petrova Street wondering how I would make it through my classes without any background in my subject areas. And how will the kids, especially the girls, react to me especially if they find out I used to be in special education? But it won't make any difference if Pop moves again.

I was awakened from my thoughts by a change in the weather. The snow, which had been falling all day, suddenly stopped, and the clouds broke up revealing the sun and the peaks of the Adirondack Mountains. It was the first time I had noticed the mountains. It was like some goofy sign. It made such an impression on me that I vowed that some day I would make the mountains a part of my life. I was startled back into reality by the sound of students honking their car horns, glad to be out of school. Me, I was just glad to be <u>in</u> school.

Chapter 39

As I sprinted up the stairs to our apartment, I didn't even have to open the door to hear the argument.

There are no jobs here, Jim! It's forty below zero! There are no jobs! I want to go back to Syracuse!

No! We're staying here! I can find work!

That's what you always say! We need to pay our bills! I'm tired of bill collectors!

We're not leaving! No wonder God never helps you!

Stunned by Pop's remark, Mom launched a tirade at him like I had never heard before. I left the room. They obviously didn't care about my day at school. So I just went to my room

As the weeks progressed, I somehow hung in there in Preliminary Science and Citizenship Education, but English and Mathematics were a struggle for me.

After the fourth week, Mrs. McKillip knew for sure that I didn't understand the math work. One day after the bell rang she cornered me before I could leave the room.

Jimmy, we need to talk! Come see me after school today.

I had a pretty good idea what she was going to say, but I was in her room immediately after school. She was grading papers as I slouched in. Peering over her glasses, she asked me to sit down in the desk in front of her. She talked quietly from her desk.

Your math skills are very poor, Jimmy. I don't understand why you are struggling so much.

I'm just having problems. I've never been good at arithmetic.

Where did you say you came from?

Oswego, but originally from Syracuse.

Didn't you learn any arithmetic skills in elementary school?

There wasn't much learning there like we do here.

Why's that?

It was a different kind of a school.

What do you mean different?

We learned lots of everyday survival skills.

Survival skills? You should have been learning math, English and other subjects. What kind of a school was it?

Reform school. Of course, I had to lie.

Reform school! Why didn't you tell me this before?

I don't know. I guess I was embarrassed.

Nevertheless, you should have told me.

I shrugged my shoulders.

Does Mr. Saint Hill know this?

I guess.

I should have been informed about this.

I guess my dad wanted to keep it quiet.

I still should have been told about your circumstances.

Yes. It would have been nice to tell her. It would have been right to tell her. But I had to keep it a secret. I couldn't explain my background. Besides, it wouldn't have made any difference. I had to get through math as well as my English class no matter what kinds of problems I had, and no matter what my background had been.

Well, Jimmy. You need to pass this class. You'll have to start coming in after school for help.

Okay. That's fine.

Starting tomorrow. Come in every day if you have to. But get in here.

And I did. As many days as I could. I had to pass this class. But I had that terrible thought again. What would happen if I didn't pass? God, I couldn't even imagine what would happen if I was held back another year! Next year I would be 16 in 7th grade! I couldn't take that.

And then, of course, we moved again. This time to South Hope Street. But at least I was still in Saranac Lake.

When I got home from school I headed to the refrigerator. Empty. No food. The only thing we had to eat was peanut butter, a loaf of bread and a quart of milk.

We don't have anything to eat Mom.

I know. Dad's had a hard time getting a job.

I made a sandwich and slouched in the chair.

What's the matter, Jimmy?

If I don't pass my subjects, I'm quitting school.

What's the problem?

It's too hard. Especially math. Half the time I don't know what she's talking about. English is like that too. I don't understand those diagrams she puts on the board. They're confusing.

You need to try harder.

Then I just snapped. I can't study any harder! I don't have enough background in math and English! I've got so much catching up to do that I'm not sure I can do it. If I don't pass this year, I'm quitting school and joining the service! Maybe I can learn some kind of a skill or make it a career. I'll be too old to repeat 7th grade. I'm not going to repeat another year at 16. Even if I do make it, how old will I be when I graduate? Nearly 21!

An education is important, Jimmy.

What are you talking about, Mom? You dropped out of school in sixth grade!

I could see that she was hurt by my remark, and I sort of regretted saying it, but I was tired of all her constant talk about how important education is in life. I knew how important. I was glad to be in regular class. But it was so damn frustrating.

Yes, but times were different. I grew up during the Depression.

By this time Pop was home, and he started in. You need an education. They can't ever take that away from you.

Pop, you're the one that always wanted me to go into the service and make it a career. You said I could learn a skill from being in the service. Besides, why didn't you two ever show an interest in my education when I was younger? When it would have been easier to do something about it? That was the end of the discussion. I left the room.

Chapter 40

A few frozen weeks later the winter slowly turned into spring. And, of course, I daydreamed in Study Hall about getting out of school for summer vacation. I was brought back to reality by the sound of the bell for the end of the day. As I walked out of the building I could see the track team warming up for practice. I stood there and watched them, thinking it would be nice to be on the team next year. Maybe I'll be fast enough to be on one of those relay teams. As I stood there, I suddenly started to feel warm and itchy all over my face and back so I headed home.

When I got to the house Mom was sitting at the table drinking her tea. She had a bottle of pills next to her.

What are those?

Tranquillizers. To calm my nerves.

Mom, I don't know what's wrong. I'm itching all over, especially my arms and stomach.

Let me see. I think you've got the measles

Measles! How could I get the measles?

It's easy. You never had them before. You're going to have to stay home from school.

I can't miss school!

Well, you're going to have to.

How long will I have to stay home?

I'm not sure. These things usually last a few days to a week.

I slouched into my bedroom and into bed. I was isolated for a week. When I got back to school I went to see Mrs. McKillip.

Where have you been? You know you can't afford to miss any school.

I had the measles.

Well, you've got lots of work to do. You'll need to get back into your routine of coming in after school.

And so I did, again. And also for English because Mrs. Alliason couldn't understand why my English was so poor, especially my writing.

Jimmy, your grammar is terrible and your writing skills are atrocious. You must learn your grammar and build your sentence structure. I don't understand how you made it this far with such poor English skills.

Of course I didn't explain my past. I just nodded my head and said, I know. I'll come in after school.

I don't know how many times over the years I had heard how behind I was. I hated diagramming sentences. I don't think I learned anything from them. I had difficulty knowing an adverb from an adjective and I could never figure out a dangling participle. About the only grammar I did learn was never to end a sentence with a preposition.

What really bothered me was that I could never find the words to describe in writing what I saw, what I wanted to say, or how I felt. But I just kept coming in for help.

The school year was nearing an end and I was in working on my math after school when three girls walked into the room.

One of them said, Now we find out that this year's teachers aren't as bad as the 8th grade teachers will be.

What about the fun stuff? For me it was meeting new boys!

Yeh. The girls were giggling.

I really liked the Christmas party.

I envied them. I wasn't there for the party or the first day of school. It must be nice to have those memories.

I took my math and English tests the last Friday of school. When Mrs. McKillip handed out the test, I immediately looked at all the problems to see if I could solve them. Taking out my scratch paper and pencil I started on the first question and worked as many questions as I could until the bell rang.

I had worked hard and had kept plugging away at my studies. And, amazingly, despite my measles, and despite math, and despite English, I passed! I busted my butt, and it paid off. Granted, I wasn't at the same level as the other kids. And, yes, I still was behind, but finally I was learning some basic skills.

When I got home Mom, Pop and Joanie were sitting down talking at the kitchen table.

Guess what?

What? Said Mom.

I passed all my classes. I go to 8th grade next year!

That's good, Jimmy.

Yeh, that's great, bud.

See, you do have the ability to do the work.

I know, Joanie, but I never had the chance to prove it before.

Now, we need to tell you something.

We're moving.

From Saranac?

No. Just to Park Avenue. I rented an upstairs apartment that's cheaper than this house.

They'll let us have Buffy.

That's good, Mom, but you better keep training him to go outside and not pee on the pillows.

I'm sorry we ever got that dog, said Pop. He's been nothing but a pain. He poured himself another glass of wine. We're moving in three days.

The last day of school Mr. Saint Hill called me into his office.

Jimmy, I see where you passed all of your classes. Barely, in math and English, but you passed.

Yes, I did.

Well, I hope you do just as well next year. You deserved to pass. Mrs. McKillip said you came in almost every day after school for help. That took a lot of sacrifice while the other kids were out having fun. Good job.

Thank you. And again, to myself, I said, thank you.

———————————

Chapter 41

After school I headed to Bernie's. A great hangout. I sat down at the counter and drank a soda. A few seats from me was a kid quietly tapping his drumsticks on the counter. We struck up conversation and he introduced himself as Tom Hennessey. He was in the drum and bugle corps.

Why don't you join? We're always looking for guys. It's not that hard and you'll have lots of fun. We meet a couple of times a week and then we go to parades during the summer.

A few days later I was a drummer. But I was having trouble learning the notes.

What's the matter? another drummer asked.

I'm having a hard time with these notes.

Let me show you. He made it seem so easy.

Why can't I do that?

You can. Hold the sticks this way. You'll get it. Just keep practicing.

Thanks for the help. I'm Jimmy Corso.

Glad to meet you, Jimmy. They call me Bunk.

When I wasn't drumming, the rest of the summer I goofed off shooting basketballs or tossing the football. One day I was up at the high school with Tom and Bunk and some other guys tossing around a football. We were right in the middle of the football field when we saw two men approaching us. One was a big guy. The other guy was smaller than me.

Hi, guys. I'm Ernie Stautner.

Damn, he's big! Do you know him Tom?

Yeh, he plays defensive line for the Pittsburgh Steelers. He's part owner of the drive-in movie here.

Yeh, we call it the passion pit, said Bunk, as all the guys laughed. I didn't laugh because I didn't understand what was so funny.

You guys are throwing the ball all wrong, said the little guy in a scraggly voice. Hold the ball this way and throw it like this. He threw the ball toward the end zone then sprinted to get it and sprinted back to us. Now when you punt the ball...

We looked at each other with a smirk on our faces, as if to say, Who is this guy?

When he was finished he tossed the ball to me and proclaimed, or exclaimed, I don't know which, I'll see you guys in two weeks. I'm your new football coach. Duke.

Two weeks later I was sitting in the bleachers with Tom Hennessy as he pointed out some of the guys from last year's team.

Those two guys at the door are our halfbacks. Big Charlie Hoffer, 175 pounds is our fullback, and the redheaded guy is our shifty halfback Billy O'Dell, 165 pounds. All those guys sitting in the front row, Wells, 190 pounds, Thomson, 210, Frenchie, 195 and next to him Moses, 195. And the biggest of them all is Tiny, 320 pounds.

God, they were big. And me? 128 pounds! Even though I should have been in the same grade as some of the juniors, I was much smaller than any of them.

Everyone got quiet as Duke introduced himself. He talked about pride, discipline and work ethic, being on time, the importance of grades, and clean practice clothes. He finished his talk with girls.

And stay away from the girls! Don't be looking at the cheerleaders during the game! They're a distraction! They're only interested in showing off their red panties! Any questions? Okay, you have fifteen minutes to hit the field.

Hit the field we did. For the next several days we did all kinds of stretches, blocks and running that made our muscles sore. After several days of this, it was time was to end practice with wind sprints. Ten forty yard wind sprints. We lined up according to the positions we played. I certainly couldn't play line, offense or defense, so I lined up with the halfbacks, the only logical place for me. I started next to the junior and senior backs as we waited for Duke's signal.

Guys, run as hard as you can to me.

When he snapped the ball we ran. Much to my surprise, I could stay up with them. After we did our wind sprints, Duke called us into a circle.

Guys, I know the weather is hot. If you need to drink water do it before practice. It's not good to drink water during practice on these hot days. It cramps your stomach.

The fourth day we put on our pads. Duke had been trying us out at many positions. For me it was some offense and lots of defense and special teams. One of the offensive drills put the backs against two linemen. When it was my turn I had to run against Thompson and Tiny Nesbitt. Taking the ball, I ran as hard as I could. The next thing I knew I was picking myself off the ground, seeing stars, wobbling back to the line.

How do you feel?

Terrible.

You'll be okay. He laughed. I'm Steve Morgan.

I'm...

I know who you are. Bunk told me about you.

They can have this halfback crap, Morgan. I'm trying out for defensive back. I'd rather hit these guys than have them hit me. Right now I have another problem. I need to see Coach about this rash I got from my jock.

After practice I went to Coach's office. I made the mistake of calling him Coach. He nearly bit off my head.

What did I say about calling me Coach! You're to call me Duke! He was very adamant.

I explained my jock problem to him and he went to get some ointment. Waiting there, I saw this poem above his desk.

I give no thought to my neighbor's birth.

Nor the way he makes his prayer.

I'll grant him a free man's place on earth, if only his game is fair.

Hey, that's a neat quote.

It's a great quote. It comes from the New York State Athletic guidebook. Here, put this on it'll take care of that rash.

Wholly sh..! This stuff burns.

It's supposed to. Next time wear shorts and a tee shirt underneath your pads.

At the end of the three weeks, Duke posted the starting lineups on the bulletin board for Saturday's game. We gathered around to see if we made the team. There was my name. Special teams and defensive safety. I was ecstatic! Things couldn't be going better. I passed 7th grade, and now I had made starting defensive safety on the varsity team. I couldn't wait to tell Mom and Pop.

When I got home I burst in the house and into the kitchen where Mom was sitting drinking her tea. She was surrounded by several sacks of groceries.

Hey, where did we get all this food?

Dad and I went to the store.

Sarcastically I asked, Where did he get the money?

He's been working.

Working where? Doing what?

Odd jobs.

Just then, Pop came into the kitchen.

I made starting safety on the varsity team.

That's great, Jimmy. When's your first game.

This Saturday.

Pop was happy. He loved football and seemed genuinely happy that I made the team. But the rest of the night he was uncharacteristically quiet and downing his booze pretty heavily. I could always tell when he had done something stupid. And this felt like one of those times. But I went to bed happy. I was finally doing something important.

The next day was Friday. I was really excited about the game on Saturday. I couldn't concentrate on my schoolwork. I had Mrs. Alliason again this year for English. Of course, I still had the same problems I had in 7th grade. My eighth grade math teacher was Mr. Peightal. Like most of the teachers he was very patient with me but never knew about my background. I went in early in the morning for extra help. He knew I was frustrated with math, but always said something that I've never forgotten. *Don't be afraid to make a mistake, that's why they have erasers on the tip of pencils.* Again I had Mr. Dorsch for Preliminary Science. My Citizen Education class was taught by a very stern and strict, and soon to be retired, Mrs. Grace Kiernan. I sat in the first seat, third row. I feared her the most.

All morning I kept thinking about the game. At lunch, as I headed down the crowded stairs to the cafeteria, I saw Mom standing at the bottom of the stairwell.

Of course, I was surprised to see her and asked her why she was at school.

Come outside and I'll tell you.

What's going on, Mom?

Dad's in jail.

Jail! Why?

You know all that food that was on the table last night?

Yeh. So?

Do you know how we've been paying the rent in the three apartments we've lived in here in Saranac?

Mom, just tell me what's going on!

Your dad bounced checks.

You said he was working!

I thought he was. And he did do some jobs. But he didn't make enough to pay for food and rent.

So he bounced checks?

Yes.

How much did he bounce?

1,700 dollars.

1,700 dollars! That's a hell of a lot of money!

That's why he's in jail. We need to go down and see him.

When we arrived at the jail the Chief of Police, Bill Wallace, met us. He opened the doors to the back jail cell so Mom could talk to Pop. I peeked in a saw Pop pacing nervously back and forth. Mom talked briefly to him then left the cell. She stayed with him and I headed back to school. Pop had done lots of stupid things, but this was the worst. He had finally gone too far. I was angry and embarrassed. This was a small town and news traveled fast. I just hoped that this wouldn't get back to the team. We were in one hell of a mess.

I didn't talk to anyone at practice. I was trying to concentrate on tomorrow's game. Duke was reviewing tomorrow's plays and special teams. After practice Morgan and I went to Bernie's, but not before stopping at the sports store to buy something I needed. When we got to Bernie's, Tiny was standing at the jukebox with the other senior linemen.

Hey, Corso, what's in the package?

I whispered, A jock.

Let me see!

I don't know what I was thinking, but in a matter of seconds he had it out of the box and was holding it high above his head yelling, Hey everybody look at what Corso just bought. The guys laughed, the girls tee-heed, and my dark Italian skin turned wine red. I was embarrassed, but it did loosen me up a bit.

When I went home it was back to reality. Pop was sitting at the kitchen table drinking his wine. Somehow they'd let him out. I couldn't sleep that night, not just because of the game, but also because of Pop's stupidity. I went into the bathroom and took one of Mom's tranquilizers so I could calm down and get some sleep.

I awoke at five, and went to school early. We boarded the bus at eight sharp, stopped at Potsdam for breakfast then headed to our game.

We did the customary warm-up drills and stretching. At game time the captains went to the center of the field for the coin toss. We lost the toss, and kicked off. I was on the kick-off team and immediately got into my position. I ran hard down the field and assisted in a tackle and then went to my position on defense. The offense snapped the ball and immediately there was a big pile of guys on the runner. I turned and went back to my position. I watched as guys went running on and off the field. I couldn't figure why the heck our offense was in a huddle. Then I heard O'Dell, our halfback, yelling at me.

Corso, what are you doing out here?

I'm playing defense. Why are you guys our here?

Then suddenly Duke is yelling at me. Get off the field!

What happened, O'Dell?

They fumbled the ball! He was chuckling at me. You can't play defense when we've got the ball!

I saw Duke frantically waving his arms for me to get off the field. I sprinted to the side thinking I was in deep poop, but to my surprise he wasn't angry at me. We went on to win the game and then took the long bus drive home. Some of us sang songs while others slept. Happy at our first victory.

Chapter 42

The following Monday after a short practice, instead of heading to Bernie's with Morgan and some of the guys, I went home. Mom was sitting at the kitchen table. Pop was talking on the phone in the next room.

I know I'm a bum, but can't you help me out? You're right, I should have thought this out before I wrote the checks, but I needed to have money for food and to pay the bills. Yes, I know I have a hard time paying back money, but I promise, I'll pay it back.

Is Pop talking to Uncle Joey?

No. He won't give us any more money. Dad never pays him back. He's talking to Aunt Margaret.

I didn't want to listen any more so I went to my room and tried to do my homework, still hoping the guys wouldn't find out what Pop did.

The next day Pop went to Western Union to get money. Three days later we moved again, to Park Avenue.

We ended the football season with four wins and three losses. Next was basketball. I tried out and made the J.V. along with Morgan, Bishop, Luce, Heck, Buckley, Beebe, and Goetz. We were the youngsters on the football team and now we were on the J.V. basketball team that was coached by Duke. I was happy and everything was going great. As I headed for practice one day I heard a guy call my name. I turned around and recognized the guy as one of the ushers at the movie show. He was a senior and I couldn't figure out why he wanted me.

Hey, how would you like to go out with a senior girl?

Is this a joke?

No, it's not. This girl wants to go out with you.

But she's a senior.

Yeh, she is, and you can meet her tomorrow before you got to practice.

I didn't give it much thought. In fact, I forgot about it because I really did think it was some kind of a joke. The next day at practice, waiting at the door was this senior guy with this girl. She was pretty and had long hair. I don't know what she saw in me, a small, dark skinned Italian. I walked like an ape, was in eighth grade, weighed about 130 pounds and was sixteen years old. Janice was nineteen.

After practice I kept wondering why she liked me. She had to be playing some kind of a joke. As I went up the stairs to our apartment a man came running down and almost knocked me over. Opening the door to the apartment, I saw Mom was crying and was visibly shaken.

What's going on, Mom? What happened?

That guy made a pass at me!

Who was he?

He delivered some end tables for the apartment. He asked me if your dad was home and I said no. Then he grabbed me and tried to kiss me. I pushed him away and said I'm not like that. He must have heard you come into the house.

Pop was so angry that it gave him an excuse not to pay the bill.

The next few weeks went along great. Janice worked in the typing department where I would meet her after practice. Somehow my hormones were more interested in her than in basketball. But I managed to keep my grades up, play basketball and go out with Janice.

As for basketball, we were learning to be tough and competitive. That's the way Duke wanted us because we would be part of the nucleus of his football team next year.

But boy, we did have some bad games. One time we were losing a game that we should have been winning. At half time Duke was so angry that he didn't come into the locker room. We didn't know what to do. When we started to go back to the second half in he walked with his jacket and hat.

Guys, I'm leaving. If you can't play better than this, then there's no sense in me coaching you. He walked out of the locker room. We stood in disbelief looking at each other.

Let him go, said Skylark, our back-up center, arrogantly laughing.

We don't need him, said Bishop. We can win this game without him.

We ran out on the court all pumped-up and won the game. Duke never left the gym. He stayed off to the side and let his assistant, Lonelli, coach the team, but Duke did get in trouble for what he did. In fact, this was the beginning of a very volatile relationship between him and the administration.

As the basketball season continued, school and love were going along great. I was working hard in school and starting on the J.V. team. Janice and I had a great time dating each other, even though she was older. I would meet her sometimes after practice in the typing room where she worked and we'd go for a long walk. On weekends we would go to the movies. We were a couple, and I had my first love.

But Mom and Pop didn't like me going out with a girl three years older and wanted me to break up with her. Fat chance unless she broke up with me. And she did. I'm sure they said something to her. January of 1957, she ended the relationship. I was crushed.

Chapter 43

A few days later we moved again. This time to McCleand Street. Even though I didn't have Janice, I still had basketball, and of course, I was still in regular class. My math grade was a C, and English had also improved to a C. Thank God, no special education classes.

But I kept feeling like I was coming down with a bad cold and a sore throat. One practice, I even had pains in my chest. Duke advised me to see a doctor. I told Mom and Pop about the pains. Two days later we were sitting in front of the desk of this very old doctor, with gray, curly hair, glasses and a bow tie. After the introductory questions, he sent me to the back room where he listened to my heart. Next, I was standing behind an

x-ray machine. Then I was lying on my back hooked up to several wires for an EKG. Then I was on the way to the hospital where a needle was inserted into my right arm to take several vials of blood. Three days later we were back sitting in front of his desk.

Jimmy's got some problems. Listening to his heart, I detected a swooshing sound, which indicates a back flow of blood through his valves. The x-rays show enlarged ventricles and irregular heartbeat, which along with his backflow of blood indicates a heart murmur. The blood test shows a high white blood cell count. Jimmy has rheumatic fever.

Mom and Pop were shocked. I had no idea what it was.

How could this have happened!

We don't know. It could be that the bacteria from his recent sore throat contributed to his condition. He probably was born with enlarged ventricles. Whatever the cause, Jimmy needs to be immediately confined to bed.

No! I can't do that. I have too much going for me!

You don't have any choice. We need to take care of this immediately or you'll be in serious condition for the rest of your life.

This can't happen! I'll be fine! I gotta go to school!

You need to be confined to bed indefinitely. You're not to get out of bed except to go to the bathroom. Plenty of fluids, fruits and vegetables. Also, aspirin will help to relieve the pain in the joints. Sulfur pills are also available.

An hour later, the second week in February of 1957, there I was, confined to bed with rheumatic fever. My only privilege was going to the bathroom.

Several days later Mrs. Siedenstein, a little Jewish woman who I became very close to over the next seven months, began tutoring me. She came in for one hour, three days a week. She did the best she could with the core subjects. But it was just another setback.

Just like special education. I was missing out on so much everyday material. The lectures, quizzes and tests, plus the class trip to Fort Ticonderoga. I missed the class trip! But that's not all I missed. I couldn't play any sports for a whole year. I became depressed. I felt cheated and was angry at everything, including God. At age sixteen, I had yet to complete a full year of school. Six years in special education, and now I had only made half a year in seventh and another half in eighth grade.

I lay in bed, morning, noon, and night. Wishing I could be anywhere except this bed. I was so bored. I hated it. I played stupid baseball games with my baseball cards. I watched stupid soap operas and Dick Clark and his "American Bandstand." At nighttime it was "Ozzie and Harriett," "Father Knows Best," and "I Love Lucy." Sitcoms that idealized the warm, closely knit family of the fifties. Yeh, sure. Hey, this is the Corso family. I tried to keep my faith by watching "Life is Worth Living" by Bishop Fulton J. Sheen. I got so tired of watching T.V. in bed that I have never, ever, done it the rest of my life.

Then there was the radio. I listened to Boom Boom Branigan, Tommy Shannon, and Dick Bianti. I actually enjoyed listening to the wisdom and insight of Paul Harvey. I was so bored I even read *Reader's Digest* and books by Billy Graham.

Duke would visit me and give me a pep talk about getting better and stronger. Sometimes, after some of the guys visited me, I would lay there for several hours, looking out the window wishing I were back in school with them. I was angry. Not just because of lying in bed, but because I couldn't play any sports. By the end of summer I was allowed to get out of bed and stay up for a few minutes. Eventually the minutes turned into hours, then, thankfully, days.

School couldn't start soon enough for me. I passed eighth grade literally laying on my back. I had to go back to the hospital for more blood tests, x-rays and EKGs, but I was allowed to go back to school. But I still couldn't play sports. It was agonizing watching the guys play. I was envious. But I had one bright spot. This time it was Barb. We had a great time, but by the end of the year, she called it off.

Chapter 44

At the age of seventeen I passed ninth grade. I finally completed one full year of school! By spring of '58 we moved again. This time to Charles Street, but still in Saranac. I was still being monitored for my rheumatic fever, but gradually I was allowed to participate in Duke's summer basketball program. I was getting stronger, and by fall I was playing football. And Barb was back. Life was good.

Then on a Tuesday morning, I found Mom at school standing at the top of the stairwell of the second floor, crying.

What's wrong?

The house caught on fire!

What do you mean it caught on fire!

That's what I mean, Jimmy! It caught on fire!

One of Mom's friends was waiting outside in the car and drove us home. When we got there the fire was under control. I got out and ran up the front stairs and upstairs to the bedrooms then back downstairs and screamed at one of the firemen.

What happened to the cat and dogs?

Two of them are there by the side of the house. The other one is tied up across the street.

I ran to the side of the house and saw Butch lying on the ground. He had died from suffocation. Butch was a stray I found last year before I got rheumatic fever. Butch and I befriended one another, and even our cat and Mom's dog Buffy loved him. Buffy and Butch were a great comfort to me when I was lying in bed all those months. Buffy somehow survived the fire. The parlor, dining room and kitchen were completely gutted. The rest of the house was smoke damaged. Many of our clothes were smoke damaged or completely burned. My hard-earned football varsity jacket and letter sweater were burned. I never replaced them. The irony of the fire was Mom watching the fire engines speed by her as she was going to the doctor's office, not knowing they were going to our house.

Chapter 45

We were scrimmaging Norwood's football team. After the first team got done running their plays, Duke put in the second team offense. I ran one play into the line, trying to spin off and backed into the lineman tackling me, but Duke saw it differently.

Corso! What the hell are you doing?

I tried to explain, but it didn't do any good. He grabbed me by my shirt and was in my face.

I don't ever want to see you back into the line again! Do you see that hill? Run over there and don't come back!

I ran over and past the hill. Angry and crying, I vowed never to play for him again. Pop saw the whole thing and came over to talk to me, telling me it was Duke's job to act like that. He was the coach and expected more from me.

I hated to admit it, but Pop was right. I learned to push myself. Not just that incident, but spending all those months in bed, made me become more determined to succeed in life.

The football season ended with a 4-3 record.

Before basketball season I had to go through my annual blood and EKG tests to make sure I was okay for basketball season. Duke had taken over the varsity team. Although I didn't start all the games, I did see lots of playing time. I was just a little playmaker setting up plays and giving the ball to our 6'5" center Mike Buckley and his brother Tim.

But Duke was up to his antics again. We weren't playing well. And, as he did the year before, during practice this time, he got so mad at us that he lined up ten basketballs and then kicked them one by one into the upstairs bleachers. We had a mediocre basketball season. The end of the basketball season was the beginning of track and another series of hospital tests.

I worked real hard at running because it was something I could do. Although I was very competitive in the 100, I was even stronger in the 220. I never got my speed up fast enough in the 100, but once I got half way into the 220, I got faster. I participated in three events in track: broad jump, the 220 and anchored the 880-relay team. By the end of the season I had my share of ribbons.

We never had an official track, we practiced on a makeshift track on the side of the school, but we still had an excellent team. In '59 we entered the Van Dusen's Northern League championships, co-favored to win with Ogdensburg. I was in the open 220. I won my morning heats and was in the afternoon final in lane three. Placing my blocks at the starting line, I was so nervous I actually was shaking and dry heaving. I tried to stay calm so I wouldn't jump the gun, but once it went off I forgot everything and just concentrated on making the curve then the straightaway. As always I was behind the other guys going into the curve, but once out of the curve, it was all me. I couldn't believe I won a gold medal. I came of age. After all I'd been through the last nine years I finally really succeeded at something. The meet was close, but our relay team never got a chance to go against Ogdensburg and determine the winner of the race and meet. We got rained out. Fountain, Cassavaugh, Bishop and me, we never got a chance to prove we could be the best in the league in the 880 relay.

Barb and I went to the prom, but by the end of the school year she broke up with me, again. We were too much alike. Moody.

But then there was something new. I had finally found a class where all of us students were beginners. Biology. I was totally fascinated with the one-celled organisms and Mr. Schroll's biology class all year. When he drew diagrams of cells, chromosomes and plants on the board he always had my attention. Even though I was in the non-regents program, biology made an impression on me for the rest of my life. At the end of the year I approached Mr. Schroll about taking the regents final instead of the non-regents.

I can't do that Jimmy? You're classified as non-regents material and must be tested in that area. It's against school policy.

But why would it make any difference?

It just would. For whatever reason, the school has placed you in the non-regents program. And that's where you will be tested. I'm sorry.

Two weeks later we had our final non-regents exam. I felt I did fairly well, especially in biology. The next day Mr. Schroll saw me walking down the hallway.

Would you like to see your test score?

Yeh. I guess.

You should be very happy Jimmy. I know it's not the regent's exam, but you scored very well. You got 93 out of 100 questions.

Of course, I was happy. Not bad for a kid whose been in special education for six years! I wanted to yell! But I didn't.

———————————————

Chapter 46

Duke's problems with the Saranac School board had been heating up during the last two months. This was his third year and everyone knew he didn't get along with the school board. His non-conformist attitude, his telling like it is to the superintendent, to the principal and to the teachers, his blowing his whistle to keep order in study hall, never set well with the administration. They fired him.

We went on strike. That was unheard of in 1959, but we did. Apparently we made the national news. Most of the football and basketball players blocked off the doors trying to prevent other students from going into the building. And it worked during the morning. But by lunchtime the administrators convinced us that he wasn't coming back, and it was to our benefit if we came back to classes it would be on our record the rest of our lives. Their scare tactic worked. Of course they were bluffing, but we went back and Duke moved on with his life, moving to Boulder, Colorado and a successful coaching career.

The school year '59-60, we had a new football and basketball coach. It was a tough year for coach Sturgeon because we were so loyal to Duke. For me, the highlight of the basketball season was the game against highly regarded Gouverneur. With the game tied, with less than thirty seconds to play I stole the ball, drove to the basket and scored, putting us briefly ahead. My only points for the game. We lost by two points.

We had an average football and basketball season. But track season would be great for me as well as the team. We always had a great track team, and that year was no different. We won all our dual meets. We were favored again going into the Van Dusen's, and our 880 relay was tops. Bishop, lead off runner in the 880 relay, and Morgan, our number two runner, were also the 100 runners. Bishop was favored to win and he did.

But the surprise was Morgan coming in second. As they were walking back to the middle of the field, one of our team came over to congratulate them and inadvertently stepped on the top Bishop's right foot, causing a severe gash, and disabling him for the 880 relay.

The other schools were happy, thinking they now had a chance to beat us, especially our archrival, Tupper Lake. After many snide remarks from their relay team, the time came for the race. Kilroy did a good job running first in place of Bishop. He handed off to Morgan. Morgan and Heck both ran hard. When I got the baton I was five yards behind Tupper Lake. But coming off the curve, as always, it was all me. I saw Anderson from Tupper ahead of me. I don't know if I was yelling or talking to myself, but whatever it was, I caught him and literally dove across the finish line to win. Mick Luce picked me up from that cinder track. I was pretty well bruised, but I was surrounded and mobbed by my teammates. It felt great. I never scored any touchdowns in football. I never scored many points in basketball, but in track I was successful. It was my short time for fame.

The next week we had the sectional 7&10 championships. Over twenty schools participated. I won two gold medals, in the 220 and the 880 relay. Bishop ran the relay as best he could. We even set a school record of 1:34.4. Not bad considering those old cinder tracks.

After the relay, Morgan and I met the girls we were dating. For me it was Diane, until mid-summer. I got dumped again. I had dated three girls seriously. All broke up with me, and yet, I suppose all three had a positive influence on me.

Chapter 47

But I still wasn't happy. My friend Steve Morgan and I had become very close over the years, and he knew something was bothering me.

What's the matter, Paisan? You should be happy.

I am.

Then why the long face?

I can't play next year. The state of New York says I'll be too old. All my life I've been too small, now I'm too old.

Too old?

Yeh, I'll be 19 and that's too old.

I lied. I'd be at least 20 but I couldn't tell him the truth. Then I would have to tell him a lot more of the truth.

And my grades. I've really been working trying to keep up my grades. I've got to figure out what I want to do with the rest of my life. Three years ago I was going to make the service my career. Now I'm thinking I want to do something else.

Like what?

I'd like to coach. Maybe track. Maybe be some kind of a teacher. Maybe P.E. But I don't know what. I like biology but that would be a very long shot.

Man, I know how frustrated you must be, especially about sports. But see how things work out this next year with your grades. Right now, just think about what you accomplished. The letters you earned in football, and basketball. And track. Look at all the ribbons and gold medals you won with only two years of track. And you had to overcome rheumatic fever to do it. Be happy.

As close as we were, and although he knew I was older, for forty years, Steve never knew about my time in special education. I kept my vow never to tell anyone.

My senior year was uneventful and disappointing. And in the end Morgan and the guys that I played sports with at Saranac went off to college.

Even more difficult than not playing sports, was trying to convince the guidance counselor that I could do college work. Sitting in front of his desk and discussing my future was a deadly debate.

I know I can do college work. I just need a chance!

You don't have good enough College Board scores!

I know that, but that doesn't mean I can't do the work!

These tests tell the colleges about your ability. Plus you're in the non-regents, non-college bound program!

So what?

My advice to you is to follow up on one of the vocational tests you took. It says here that you are good with your hands. You can become a clerk or work as a carpenter. Something in that area.

I don't want that kind of work!

Then, Jimmy, what would you like to do?

I want to go to college and be a coach or some kind of a teacher! The snide expression on his face and the slow shaking of his head back and forth, saying no, made me so angry. He was almost snickering. Leaning forward in his chair, he looked me straight in the eye.

A teacher?

Yeh.

What kind of a teacher?

I don't know. I like biology. And I did well on my final, even if it was non-regents.

He pulled out my transcripts and looked at them.

Yes, you did do well biology. And you even did well in chemistry. But they are non-regents classes. For non-college bound students. No college in this state will accept you with a non-regents background. You're not college material!

I'm just as smart as anyone! I know I have had some trouble in the past. But that doesn't mean I can't do college work!

Jimmy, you are not as well trained as the other students. You don't have the background. You're not college material! You won't get into a four-year college, let alone a New York State college. If you really want to try college then I'd advise you to try one out of state and see what they say.

I got up and left. End of counseling session.

I did take his advice and tried an out of state college, East Strosburg in Pennsylvania, but they rejected me. I didn't go back into his office the rest of the year. I couldn't face him. I wanted to prove he was wrong, but so far he was right. So I did the next best thing, I applied and got accepted and Paul Smith's Junior College about fifteen miles out of Saranac lake. It was an excellent college for hotel management, forestry and biology.

Even though I was going somewhere, and I was going to continue my education, the rest of the year I just pouted. It was a few weeks away from the senior prom, but I wasn't interested in going until I was coaxed into going on a blind date. That's how I ended my senior year, a blind date.

The final issue of the Red and White newspaper was published especially for the senior class. Under Senior Wills, they said I was willing my vast math knowledge to an underclassman. It was a joke, they were teasing. But for me it wasn't funny. This comment hurt. Sure, I had struggled with math, but they never knew it was because I never had any math in elementary school.

At least in Senior Superlatives I was voted best dancer. I have always wondered about that. And the best blue eyes. That was kind of cool, but they also voted me Most Moody. They were right. Although it was spelled incorrectly in Canaras, the yearbook, my nickname was Paisan, The Friendly Wop. Finally, in Senior Quotes, they saw me as "Jimmy Corso, he wishes not to be seen, but to be the Best." How true. Thank you classmates.

On June 23, 1961, nearly 21 years old, I graduated from Saranac Lake High School.

Chapter 48

The summer after graduation I got a job working at Swift's meat packing company. We started at five in the morning and worked until five in the evening. Sometimes us younger guys even went on the trucks as helpers. Then we worked until eight, only getting enough sleep to be at work at five the next morning. But I loved working with those guys so much that I stayed four summers to earn enough money to help pay my college bills.

The fall of '61, I started at Paul Smith's. Being a freshman, I was supposed to wear one of those beanies. But I wouldn't be seen dead in one of those things, so I told the upper classmen who approached me that it was my second year there. They looked at me suspiciously, but they bought it, letting me off the beanie hook.

I ran on the cross-country team. It was different from being a sprinter. The training, the running pace, the wooded running trails, and the races. Because of my intense personality and the short explosive runs from sprinting, I struggled with the longer distances. Coach Norton sensed this and would sometimes run beside me during practice, encouraging me and telling me I was doing a good job. Somehow I managed to earn a letter.

Academically, I took all the standard courses. My favorite was Zoology, taught by pipe smoking Mr. Simkins. The first day of class he explained to us the best way, in his opinion, to take notes.

Taking notes is one of the most difficult tasks in college. The best way to learn biology terms is to copy down two or three key words. That should give you enough information to help you understand what you have learned without memorizing lots of information.

I tried to do what he said in all my classes, but I was so neurotic about learning the material that I would copy down, verbatim, nearly every statement every professor said. I should have used a tape recorder.

Even though Simkins said it didn't, Zoology did require a lot of memorizing. And memorize I did. In fact, on one major test on classification only four of us scored well. He was so pleased with us that he gave each of us twenty-five cents for coffee and donuts and dismissed us early from class, while the rest of the students had to stay. As always, I worked hard at my weaknesses: math and English. It wasn't easy. But I just kept studying.

I tried basketball. I got cut in the second round. Enough said about that. The following week, I tried wrestling. That lasted one day. I got my head caught and crushed in some guy's forearms that looked like tree stumps. Enough said about that.

I passed all my classes that year and headed immediately back to Swift's to earn enough money for my second year. But there wasn't enough work, so I didn't earn enough during the summer for my second semester at Paul Smith's. Tuition and books were more expensive than I realized, and I overspent during the first semester, so I asked Pop for some help.

You'd think I was asking for his blood. I thought he was happy for me making it through my first year of college, and I think he was, as long as he didn't have to pay for it. Pop had started working for, and now actually owned a branch of, the Hudson Paper Company in Saranac. He distributed paper products, toilet paper etc., to local businesses.

I'll see, Jimmy. Let me talk to the people at Paul Smith's.

Which he did, but not until a week before the start of the new school year.

Only he didn't tell me. I finally asked him again about some help.

I already made arrangements, he said, sarcastically. They'll deduct what's left of your bill from the products I give them! I'm losing money on this. I hope you appreciate what I've done for you!

How ironic, I thought for the umpteenth time in my life. Here's a man who doesn't pay his bills, drinks his money away and loses more money in poker than it would have ever cost me at Paul Smith's. He wants me to feel, what? Guilty.

How about this? In the spring of '59, he had forged my signature on a seventy-dollar income tax return check from the IRS, from my summer job, so he could buy things. He never told me about it until I started wondering why I never received my check. I never asked for his help again.

The second year at Paul Smith's was just like my first. Hard work. I knew I had to be making some decisions soon because this was a junior college. There wasn't another year. I desperately wanted to go to an in state college, especially a teachers' college. I waited as long as I could to apply because I wanted the colleges to see my spring grades. But I also needed some recommendations.

I started with Duke, and he gave me a good recommendation for Brockport because he knew some coaches at the college. I sent in my junior college transcript, as well as my high school transcripts. Then it was the anxious wait for their response.

But I didn't stop there. Billy O'Dell was playing football for Ithaca College and was well respected as an athlete. I went with him for an overnight trip to Ithaca. He set up an interview with the admission director. We talked about my grades, the fact that I was in a non-regents program, and that my College Board scores were low. Billy stayed with me for the complete interview. Another anxious wait for their response.

Then I went to Mr. Charles Murphy, my high school principal. He knew the director of admissions at Potsdam. He also set up an interview for me that turned out to be very interesting. After much small talk, the admissions representative pulled out my transcripts and looked at them:

I'll be honest with you, Jimmy. This is not going to be easy. Even though your high school grades were above average, in biology and chemistry, they were in the non-regents program. That's non-college material.

Can't you give me a chance? I've worked hard and I know I can do the work. I've done well at Paul Smith's.

It's not just me, Jimmy. There's a committee that does the selection process.

All I need is a chance. I know colleges let in other guys because of athletics. And their grades aren't even as good as mine.

You may be right, but that's a different story.

If they get a chance, why can't I? That's not fair.

It's not that easy, Jimmy. Your college boards are not the best. In fact, they probably hurt your chances more than your grades in high school or Paul Smith's will help you.

We shook hands and I headed back to Saranac, just hoping I would get a chance at any college in the state, just a chance to prove myself.

I also applied to Oswego and Plattsburg State Teachers College and Cortland, a private college.

I heard first from Cortland. The letter started with something like, Thank you for your interest in our school, however, we feel that you don't meet the academic requirements for admittance to our program.

Next, I heard from Oswego. Thank you for your interest in our school, but we feel you don't meet the academic standards for our school.

Then Plattsburg. Same story.

I still hadn't heard from the three schools that I had had direct help in applying to: Ithaca, Potsdam and Brockport. I was down, but I still had hope. For the moment, I needed to concentrate on my final exams at Paul Smith's.

Walking across campus, deep in thought about getting into just one of these colleges, I heard a voice calling me.

Hey, Corso, where you going?

It was one of the guys in my zoology class. He was happy, almost giddy-like happiness.

I just got accepted to Brockport!

Where?

Brockport.

A cold shiver ran up my spine. I didn't say anything to him about my application to Brockport. He was in. I had seen him cheat with "crib notes" in several of his classes. He always got higher scores, and he knew I had seen him cheat, but we never acknowledged it to each other, and I never said anything. He was in. I wasn't.

The next day, after taking my Earth Science exam, I headed home and checked the mailbox. Nothing. When I entered the house, I saw the letter on the dining room table. The upper left hand corner said Ithaca College. I was nervous, my hands shook. I quickly opened the letter. I read the first two sentences. Then I got that empty, sick feeling in my stomach. We're sorry, but after much consideration, your grades don't... I stopped reading. I felt sick, but I still had hope for the other two colleges. Besides, I didn't have time to mope around. I had a math test left to take to finish up at Paul Smith's.

The next day I studied hard for math. I took a break and went to Bernie's, then came home. On the dining room table I saw the letter from Potsdam. Dear Mr. Corso, thank you for your interest in our school, but... Again I didn't finish the letter. This time I crumpled the paper and threw it away.

Two days later I received my letter from Brockport. I had that same sick feeling in my stomach. Maybe because I knew what it was going to say. I wasn't even nervous when I opened it. In fact, I was cynical, saying to myself, you probably got rejected. Dear Mr. Corso, thank you for your interest in our school. However…I didn't read the rest of it. I didn't even crumple it. I shred it to pieces. I no longer cared. There wasn't any sense in taking my math final. It was useless. I didn't show up. I walked away. I never graduated from Paul Smith's.

———————————————

Chapter 49

I was mentally down. I didn't know what I was going to do. I guess my high school counselor was right. I couldn't get into a New York state college. I couldn't even get into an out of state college.

During that summer I worked long hours at Swifts, from five in the morning, putting in twelve hour days. I hardly got a chance to see any of the guys from high school. It was August, and I had to make some major decisions about my life. I didn't know what I was going to do. My old friends seemed to know exactly what they were going to do with their lives.

After leaving work one day, I decided not just to go home for supper and crash on the couch for the night, which was my usual after work habit. I hadn't seen Steve Morgan all summer, so I decided to stop by his house and hope he was home from work. He was just getting out of his car when I got to his house.

Hey, Paisan. Where you been all summer?

Working. I'm doing twelve-hour shifts.

He laughed. Other than that, how's your summer been going?

Not good, Steve. I guess I'm headed to Syracuse to get a job. Do something. I don't know what. Maybe join the service. It's still not too late to join. I'm a little old, but it will give me some kind of a future.

What about college?

That's a joke. It's not going to happen. I can't get in. I applied to six in-state and one out of state. Every one of them rejected me. There's no hope.

Come on in the house. Let's talk.

We sat down at the kitchen table with his mom.

Jimmy, we haven't seen you all summer.

I've been busy, Mrs. Morgan.

Jimmy's leaving for Syracuse, Mom.

Why's that, Jimmy?

I can't get into college. I've tried, but I can't get any college to give me a chance. I know I can do the work. I just need a chance to prove myself. Mr. Murphy, Billy O'Dell, and Duke all tried to get me into a school, but it hasn't done me any good. I guess my past finally caught up with me.

What do you mean by that, Paisan?

Nothing. Just an inside joke with myself.

Paisan, why don't you come to Greeley with me? It's a great teacher's college. It's not easy. The classes are not pushovers. You'll have to work hard. The only other hard part is getting by the smell.

What smell?

The feedlots outside of town. It's a cow town. But it's a pretty campus. You'll love it.

What makes you think I can get in there after being rejected by colleges in my own state?

I'll call Greeley. I know the director of admissions. They're two hours behind us, so someone will still be in the office. Let's see what they say.

He was on the phone and in a matter of minutes talking to the director of admissions. When he hung up, he looked at me.

Pack your clothes. They want to interview you. There's no guarantee, but because you have been in junior college for two years, you might have a chance. Whatever the case, go out there and see what they have to say. You've got nothing to lose.

Three weeks later, and three weeks before the start of school, not even knowing if I was accepted, I said good-bye to Mom and Pop, broke my Italian strings, and headed west on a train to the little cow town of Greeley, Colorado.

The first two days on the train were long and bumpy. I tried to get as much sleep as I could, but it was hard. On the third morning, I woke up just as the sun was rising on the plains. Just as I was struck by the beauty of the mountains in Saranac Lake, I was struck by the beauty of the grasslands of Colorado. As the train got closer to Greeley, I could see the Rocky Mountains to the west. If the Adirondacks were beautiful, the sharp peaks of the Rocky Mountains were spectacular. Even if I didn't get accepted, I knew I would love it out here.

Morgan met me at the train station. He was already at school doing two-a-day practices for football.

We lived in a basement apartment with six other guys he knew from Northeastern Junior college. The next morning he showed me the administration building while he went to football practice.

I walked into the office and introduced myself to the secretary.

Hi. I'm Jimmy Corso. The director of admissions is expecting me.

She looked on her desk at some papers and then at her calendar.

Who did you say you were?

Jimmy Corso. My friend Steve Morgan talked to someone here several weeks ago about me coming out here to school. I had my high school and college transcripts sent here. They should have arrived by now.

Please have a seat. I'll be with you shortly.

I sat down and waited and thought, here I go again. What will it take for me to get into college? Finally she came out.

I'm sorry it took so long, Jimmy. We do have your papers. The school has decided to let you in on probation. However, you will have to start as a freshman. They will not accept your course work from Paul Smith's.

Why not?

They didn't say.

I knew she was lying, but what the heck, at least I was getting a chance. Even if I was a twenty-three year old freshman.

What are you declaring as your major?

Biology! I want to be a biology teacher! I said it proudly. And I want to coach!

I had to fill out some papers. Then I took off to find the football field to tell Morgan. I was overjoyed. I wanted to jump up and down. Scream, yell and holler out loud. Anything to show my pleasure. I was in the system!

I found Jackson field, but couldn't pick out Morgan because they all had on their pads and helmets. So I waited in the bleachers. I was euphoric. But then all of a sudden I had this weird feeling. What am I doing out here? All my family is back east. I'm without family and don't know anyone here except Morgan. I couldn't believe I was two thousand miles from Saranac Lake. Even though Greeley was giving me my chance, I still wondered, what am I doing out here? I keep telling everyone I can do the work. I have my chance. Now it's put up or shut up.

Chapter 50

I saw her from the balcony standing by herself on the dance floor. It was the night of the first day of classes, and it was the get acquainted dance. She was wearing a pink and white sweater, which she filled out nicely. Her blond hair was in a flip with the typical bangs of that time. I approached her nervously, thinking she wouldn't dance with me.

Hi. Would you like to dance?

Her light blue eyes stared at me for a moment.

Yes. I'd love to. This drunk keeps asking me to dance. Maybe he'll stop if he sees me dancing with you.

I'm Jimmy Corso.

I'm Karren Sechler. And judging by your accent you must be from the East.

Yes. New York. Originally from Syracuse, but I graduated from Saranac Lake.

Where's that?

It's a beautiful little place, about six thousand people, upstate, in the heart of the Adirondack Mountains.

We danced a few more times then I left for the night.

The next day was Sunday I was drinking my morning coffee at a local restaurant, reflecting on my past school years. I kept hearing a little voice inside my head asking, "Did you go to church today?" I would hear that voice almost every Sunday while I was in college. And no matter how down I felt, I always managed to go to church. I'm not sure how much it helped me, but like everything I did in my life, I made it a habit. I was looking forward to tomorrow, to starting my new classes, especially biology. I wasn't taking a full load, which meant, if I made it that far, I probably wouldn't graduate until the winter of '67.

"Don't you know?" Often, DR. Stamper would make a biological statement, then end his sentence with, "Don't you know?" The class was Zoology I. Even though I never finished at Paul Smith's, I know that taking Mr. Simkins' biology class there prepared me for Zoology, as well as for the rest of my classes at Greeley.

Maynard Stamper, professor of biology. A gentleman's gentleman. I came to admire and love this professor. One day after class I was startled when he approached me.

Jimmy, I know that's not a Colorado accent. It sounds like you're from New York.

Yeh, originally from Syracuse. Is it that noticeable?

Yes, it is. Especially when I hear you say words like "water". He laughed, good-naturedly. What are you doing all the way out here in Colorado?

Breaking strings from my Italian family. I wasn't willing, and for sure still ashamed, to tell him I couldn't get into a college in my own state. After the mid-term test he approached me again.

You did well on your test, Jimmy. Not bad for a New Yorker!

Yeh. If I can get a B on your final that'll help me out of probation. I accidentally let it slip out, but in a way I was glad. I needed someone to talk to. And what finer person than this friendly gentleman?

As we walked slowly down the stairs and out the doors of the old Cranford Science building, I explained my trouble getting into college and how I finally came to Greeley. When we got to the Y in the sidewalk he stopped and looked at me.

Do you have a counselor, or someone working with you to help you?

No.

Well, son, I admire your perseverance. If you need any help, or have any problems, you come see me. He called me son, not the impersonal name "bud," that Pop used, and I hated.

And I did go see him. And I owe him a lot. He was there for me during all my years at Greeley.

Of course, I struggled in my English class, but Zoology, Chemistry and History were fine. I made it through the first semester in fine shape and was off probation.

The second quarter, I took Zoology from Bert Thomas, who I also told about my background, at least from high school on. It was in this class that I hooked up with six foot five, Bill Hakonson, eventually my best man at my wedding, who encouraged me to join a fraternity called the TEKE's. I was reluctant, but agreed to pledge because I felt it might help me relate better to people.

None of my classes were easy, but Inorganic Chemistry was the most challenging. As always, I was overwhelmed by the amount of notes I had to take for my classes and the amount of time I had to study. It wasn't minutes, it was hours and hours. I really had to burn the midnight oil to keep up my grades and stay off probation. But again I made it through the quarter.

Then I slipped a little. I was a pledge for the TEKE's, and dating a girl from Littleton. My third quarter science classes were Botany I and Organic Chemistry. All of this made for a difficult quarter. During Hell Week for the fraternity, we were up every night until two in the morning, had to wear itchy gunny sacks under our clothes every day, not get caught sleeping during the day, and attend all our classes, or feel the wrath of the brothers.

I tried. I desperately wanted to be in this fraternity, stay with my girlfriend, and pass Organic. Something had to give. During Hell Week we had a major test. The test blew me away. I couldn't recover after Hell Week and make up all that I missed from not paying attention in class. I was okay in the rest of my classes, but I just couldn't cut it in Organic. I would have to take it again, some other quarter.

Chapter 51

Spring quarter was over, and I took my three-day train trek back east. Because Mom and Pop had moved back to Syracuse, I had to find a job there. Going back to Swift's up north wouldn't be financially wise. I took a job at Crucible Steel, grinding steel, working all kinds of shifts. The midnight to eight was the most difficult, but they paid good money.

That summer I found out that New York had what they called Rockefeller Loans. I could borrow a certain amount each year I was in college. I signed a contract saying I would pay back the loan when I graduated. And I did pay it back, all of it, which eventually gave me AAA credit and allowed me to get a good mortgage on my first home.

The fall of '64 came and I was back in Greeley with my college sweetheart and, most importantly, with no problems in my classes. But now I had to keep up my G.P.A. so I could be accepted into the teacher education program.

I got a job working as a hasher, washing dishes, for one of the sororities. I got free meals so I didn't have to buy food. By the end of the school year my sweetheart and I had separated. Her parents didn't like me: I was Catholic. Italian. From New York State. Had no future. At least they never knew I had been in special education.

Over the summer, I had turned my interest to distance running, and by fall I was in good enough shape to make the varsity cross-country team. I wasn't good enough to beat the top two runners on our team, but I could hold my own at number three or four. We did our own coaching and trained ourselves. Seems our coach, who was also an assistant football coach and head track coach, was more interested in football than in the cross-country team that he was assigned to coach.

One Friday night at The Library, our local 3.2 beer place, I was standing talking to some of the cross-country guys when I felt a tap on my shoulder.

How you doing?

After a second look I recognized her as the girl I had met two years ago at the get acquainted dance.

I'm fine. I'm sure I had a surprised look on my face. I couldn't believe she remembered me. We talked for a while, then danced.

What have you been doing for the last two years?

I met a boy, we were engaged to get married. But it didn't work out. What about you?

I met this girl, we got pinned. Even got serenaded by my fraternity brothers. I thought it would work out, but her parents didn't like me. Whatever the reason, she broke off our relationship. Hey, would you like to go out tomorrow night?

No. I'm going skiing for the weekend.

What about next week?

No. I'm going skiing next weekend too.

I didn't say anything else. I figured she just wasn't interested in me.

But I'll be free the weekend after that!

Two kids and several grandchildren later, Karren still says, no, laughing at me, when I ask her out.

That spring I ran track and was finally accepted into the teacher education program. Coach Rossi, the gymnastics coach, got me a job mowing lawns for the school during the summer. This enabled me have money to travel to Wheat Ridge to see Karren.

Remarkably, my junior year came and went with no problems.

My senior year had two obstacles. Organic Chemistry and where would I do my student teaching?

Because student teaching assignments took a long time to set up, I started during the winter of '67, working with the director of student teachers. Since I was from out of state I didn't have any local high school connections. After taking the advice of Paul Richards, a biology teacher at the local school who worked with the college to help place prospective biology teachers, I applied to Wheat Ridge High School in Jefferson Country.

Now it was the waiting game again. It was spring quarter, and I was in Organic Chemistry again. Talk about working hard. I was ready to be out of school and was no longer interested in the fraternity. I was too busy with real life. I was engaged and working mowing lawns. I was also taking a full load of classes and anxious to get my teaching career started, get married and start my family.

As usual, I burned the midnight oil. I knew I could pass Organic, but I wanted more than to just get by with a D. I wanted a C or higher. Every day after class I rewrote my notes then studied them. When I took the final exam I felt pretty good about passing. When the grades came out, I got a 78%, which translated, into a C. A strong C, but on my transcript a C. I had completed my science requirements, and now all that was left was student teaching.

To my surprise, I was assigned to Highlands High School in Adams County. After I read the letter, I went to the director of student teachers, and asked why I didn't get Wheat Ridge High School.

Sometimes these things don't work out, Jimmy.

But I know they have an opening for a student teacher in biology.

They also have this opening at Highlands. You'll like it there. I've already talked to Ron Ratkovich. He will supervise you.

I still don't understand why I can't go to Wheat Ridge. Paul Richards said Ray Bolin is a good teacher and he would be great to work with.

Sometimes we have to place students where we think they will fit in. In your case it is Adams County.

I don't follow you. What does fitting in have to do with it?

Students with the highest grades get better choices. These things are out of my hands. Let's just leave it at that.

My grades weren't good enough for Jefferson County? That's what he implied. If my grades were good enough to qualify for the student teacher program, then why weren't they good enough for Jefferson County?

In the summer of 1967, Karren and I got married, and that fall I reported to Highlands High School. Not to one, but to two, supervising teachers. Ron Ratkovich and Roger Driver. I was really nervous, but still I felt confident I could do a good job. Yes, I made some mistakes. That's why there's student teaching. My number one goal was always to make sure the kids enjoyed coming to my class. That was true, not just for student teaching, but for my entire teaching career. During my student teaching I improved continually and did an excellent job, so much so that Ron tried to get me on his staff for the next school year.

I graduated from the University of Northern Colorado in Greeley on December 13, 1967. Only I knew how really happy I was. No one in Colorado, not even Karren, knew what I had gone through to get to this moment. As they called my name, I slowly walked up to the stage, enjoying every second of it. I wanted to shout. I wanted to tell my story. But I didn't. When I received my diploma, I looked out in the audience. Mom and Pop's faces were missing. I clutched my diploma case hard, opened it, and read it as I headed back to my seat. James A. Corso, Jr., Bachelor of Arts.

———————————

Chapter 52

I applied for teaching jobs in Denver, Adams and Jefferson counties to be a full time or substitute teacher. I set up interviews for all three counties. For some reason Denver never called me.

I subbed in Chemistry at Wheat Ridge High School. I found it ironic that I couldn't student teach there, but I could sub there. One day, as I was leaving at the end of school, the secretary handed me a note. It was from Jefferson County's Director of Personnel. I immediately called him, and he asked me if I was interested in teaching Life Science at North Arvada Junior High. And can you coach wrestling? Of course I didn't know anything about coaching wrestling, but that didn't make any difference. I could learn.

The next day I went up to North Arvada for my interview. If I got hired this would be better than we hoped because I was expecting to end up in one of the rural schools outside of Denver. And that would have been fine with us.

Principal Carl Zerger greeted me. He hired me. I had missed the deadline for a full year teacher's contract by one day, so he had to hire me as a substitute teacher. But I didn't care. I was happy. I had a teaching position. I was taking the position of Jim Duetch who had been drafted into the service. How ironic that I was taking his place. I was 27 years old and had never been called into the service. Because he was younger than I was, he was drafted. I guess finally it was okay to be older.

On January 2, 1968, I walked into room B-8 at North Arvada Junior High School and began my thirty-year teaching career. Because it was the middle of the year, and I was replacing a popular teacher the kids had started the school year with, I was in a very difficult position. Not only with the kids, but also with many of teachers who taught on the seventh grade level. I wanted the kids to like me and enjoy coming to my class, but I also wanted them to work hard. I wanted to tell them my story, but I felt that if they knew I had been in special education, it might backfire on me. So I never told anyone about my background.

In the spring when I went in for my evaluation, Mr. Zerger shocked me and said I wouldn't be helping with wrestling next year because the coach felt I didn't do a good job coaching. No surprise there, I was just learning the coaching ropes. And he knew I didn't have any experience before I started coaching with him. I had been up front and told everyone involved that I had never wrestled. I was really down because I had been honest. The coach never talked to me, he just stabbed me in the back and went directly to the principal.

The summer of 1968 I entered graduate school at Greeley and worked on my Master's degree in Science Education, with an emphasis in Biology. Every day, during every summer from 1968 to 1972, I traveled sixty miles to Greeley for classes. One of the highlights of my program was getting an A in Entomology, taught by Dr. Gerald Schmidt, a well-respected Parasitologist, who taught a most difficult course in Entomology.

In the summer of '72, I prepared myself for my Master's comprehensive exams. I don't know how many hours I studied for the test. Day and night, night and day, weeks and weeks. I attended every review session.

The day for the big test finally arrived. I'd taken many tests, but nothing was as important as the next two mornings. I wrote for four hours each day. I know my English was not the best, but my knowledge of the science was very strong. Then again it was the big wait. Sometimes, it seems like that's all I ever did. Wait for responses. From getting out of special education, to getting into college, to finishing my master's program. Wait and see. The big wait.

I've always been nervous waiting, but this was the worst. I couldn't even bear the thought of not getting my Master's. I needed it to advance on the pay scale.

On July 28, 1972 I received my letter. I was nervous. Real nervous. I opened it quickly, but read it slowly, savoring every word, especially the words: Congratulations, you have successfully passed the written comprehensive exam. I was ecstatic! In 1963, I couldn't even get into a four-year college, now here I was ready to walk up the aisle and receive my Master's degree.

On August 12,1972, exactly five years after the day of my marriage. I listened for my name, then walked down the aisle to get my diploma. Again nobody knew what I had accomplished. I still had no one to share my great sense of accomplishment. I had never even told Karren. From scoring a 70 on that test and being labeled as retarded to getting my master's degree. I thought about Miss Towne, Chucky, Eddie, and those six years in special education.

Outside, I had a big smile on my face. Inside, I was crying out with joy. I had made it.

Other than my marriage and the birth of my kids, this was the proudest day of my life. But as I received my diploma and looked out into the audience, again Mom and Pop's faces were missing.

Chapter 53

It was a cold, November morning in 1980. I was at 7500 feet and starting down the mountain trail at White Ranch outside Arvada, when I saw him coming up the trail. I could see the cold air coming from his nostrils. Twitching his long ears and short tail, he ran effortlessly over the uneven rock trail as if he had done it all his life. He spooked a bit and veered off to the side of the trail.

His running partner was Lee Courkamp, an outstanding runner in college and road racing. I could see Lee didn't want to stop to talk right then, so I continued my descent. I knew Lee was an avid runner and coach, but I had no idea why he was running up the mountain with a burro.

Anxious to find out what they were doing, I waited for them in the parking lot. After they finished their run, I ran up to the horse trailer and stopped behind the donkey.

Hey, don't get behind him! yelled Lee. He'll kick you so hard you won't walk for a week!

What's his name?

Samson. He's two years old. I just adopted him from the Grand Canyon.

What are you up to with him?

I race with him and my other donkey in the burro races over Mosquito Pass.

Would you like to practice with him sometime?

Yeh. I'd like that. It would sure be something different.

Ok. Good. Come over to Coates' pasture next Saturday morning at 7:00. It's the safest time of day to run with him. If the weather is nice, we'll go for a short seven-mile run. The pasture is a little west of the Dairy

Queen on Ralston Road. If you like running with him, you can get in the first race at Fairplay the last Sunday in August.

And so started my relationship with Samson and our journey into the thirty-mile pack burro races held in the Colorado mountains at Fairplay, Leadville and Buena Vista.

But it wasn't easy. During one of the training sessions Samson kicked me so hard in the groin that I was unable to run for a week, not to mention what that kick did to my married life for a while. But, like everything else in my life, I decided to just keep plugging away. I bought Samson from Lee for a few bucks. My mother-in-law, Verna, let me keep in him her corral, which made it easy for me to train him.

The races are thirty miles long, starting at an elevation of 10,000 feet. Legend has it that the old-time miners raced their donkeys over the passes to see who would be the first into the next community.

The donkeys must carry a backpack of 33 pounds with a saddle, shovel and miner's pick and a fifteen-foot lead rope. The runner and the donkey must run together as a team, never losing contact with each other. If you do separate as a team, you must go back to the spot where you separated from each other and start again from that point. The team races to the 13,000 foot summit Mosquito Pass, goes past the plaque that honors the priest that carried mail over the pass to the mining communities, then starts its long journey back down the mountain to Fairplay and Leadville.

The reward? A few bucks to feed your running partner for a year and a small trophy buckle with a picture of a donkey engraved on it.

I had a good three years with Samson. I have always loved running. The feel of it. The movement of my muscles, the breathing, the rhythm of my body. Running with Samson was even better because we trained on the streets, trails and in the mountains in the cool of the morning. For Samson it was probably like running back in the Grand Canyon. For me, as always, it was a great escape, a release of my constant nervous energy.

Running with Samson was a great experience until one fateful August Sunday at Fairplay. We were running great as a team. The lead team of Ardel Boes and burro Billy were ahead of the pack by the time we got to American Flats, near the 12,000-foot level. Samson and I reached the top and went past the plaque and then headed down the mountain. About 100 yards into our descent, I tripped and hit my right knee on a rock. I couldn't move. I had never felt any pain like it before. I got up and tried to run, but I collapsed on the ground. The next thing I remember I had ice packs on my leg and I was in the back of a four-wheel-drive pick up truck going down the mountain and into the local hospital where they rushed me to x-ray.

What happened? asked the doctor.

I'm a burro racer.

You don't need to tell me any more. I live up here so I know how you guys train and run.

It's my knee. I can't move it. Look at the size of it!

It doesn't look good. What's your name?

Jimmy.

Well, Jimmy. I'll take an x-ray and let you know what's going on.

The next hour went by slowly as the nurse monitored my vital signs. I was really hurting. The doctor finally came back with the results.

You smashed most of your right knee. You will need to see a specialist in Denver. The truth is most of it will have to be removed. I'm afraid your running career is over.

I laid my head back on the pillow. It was Saranac Lake all over again. Another setback. Only this time I couldn't overcome the physical obstacle of a missing right knee. Angier than ever. I thought I made peace with my God.

I was never really the same. Emotionally or physically. I have to wear a brace when I run. But, even today, I still manage to get in thirty miles a week.

Chapter 54

Thirty years of teaching really goes by fast. Does that mean I enjoyed it? Yes. I had a very interesting career with the usual highs and lows. However, after thirty years, it was time to move on.

During the last ten years, I found myself working harder than most of the kids. If it was difficult, they just gave up. I wanted to shake them. I wanted to tell them my story. To tell them, Stop quitting! You can accomplish anything within your ability. I did. Perseverance and work ethic will pay off. You just have to do it. No excuses. And, maybe I should have told them.

On my retirement day, I thought back on my roller coaster teaching career. I thought about my first day in January of 1968 at North Arvada Junior, standing there looking out at those seventh graders and wondering, Where my career will go? Getting fired as wrestling coach that year balanced with 1972, when I was head wrestling coach at North Arvada and we went undefeated in our dual meets. Not bad for a guy who a few years earlier was relieved of his duties.

Then there was the 1973, low point when I was ejected from a wrestling match for arguing with the referee. Then two parents that had had too much to drink came out of the stands and charged the referee. A fight ensued between them, the referee and some opposing fans. I was suspended from coaching because the administration said I was at fault for the fight.

But in fall of 1974, with the recommendation from Jim DePaulo, I was hired by John Musciano, principal of Bear Creek High School, as a cross-country coach and biology teacher.

What a great school! Under the leadership of Jimmy Mitchell, the biology department was well organized, not only in preparation of classroom materials, but also in the team teaching concept that we developed. Bear Creek set the foundation for me for my next twenty-four years of teaching.

And that fall of '74 I had the number one and number two sophomore cross-country runners in Jefferson County. I had one of the best cross-country teams in the state. It really felt good having such a competitive team. We won some invitational meets and were ranked in the top ten in the state. I had a great feeling that we would do well, and that year I was really on a high. But a rule change, which was reversed a couple of years later, deprived my team of a chance to run at state that year. I was soured on cross- country, and when my two runners quit because it was too frustrating and too hard, I gave up too.

But then in 1977, as head wrestling coach, we won the Poudre Valley Invitational, just missed third place in the district meet, and two of my wrestlers, Don Caudle, county champion at 112 pounds, and Frank Carmody, at 132, competed at the state meet. Both placed fourth in state.

Up and down the roller coaster went, at least the coaching roller coaster. In 1980, tired of the long drive to Bear Creek High, I had transferred to Arvada High School. In 1983, head football coach Jim Bratten asked me to coach his sophomores. That was the year I shattered my right knee at the burro races on top of Mosquito Pass. With one leg in a cast, I did my best to coach the kids. They nicked named me Gimpy. I coached for the next four years.

One day in 1987, I unaccountably found myself in the principal's office with the school lawyer defending me in a lawsuit from a former football player who was injured in the fall of 1984. I couldn't even remember what happened this fall, let alone what happened three years ago. Even though I eventually was exonerated, I was emotionally down. Soured and bitter by the lawsuit, which delved into my private life and my character, I quit coaching permanently.

In fall of 1987, I took over the Biology II program at Arvada and found myself teaching college-bound students. Not bad for a non-regents, non-college bound kid.

Chapter 55

In 1990, Pop came to Colorado. He lived with us a while, but of course, it turned out to be a disaster. We tried to establish rules before he moved in. But it was like growing up with him all over again. Eventually I found an apartment that the government subsidized for low-income people. It was a nice, clean building that provided lots of activities for senior citizens, but Pop wouldn't make the adjustment. He just moped and pouted about his existence. It was beneath him. But he and I just couldn't live under the same roof anymore.

At the end of the 1997 school year, worn out from dealing with Pop, and tired of school and long weekends and after-school hours working my lawn and vending machine businesses, I retired from teaching. I was burnt out. I had had a good run, but I was done.

On the last day, of February 1998, I went to Pop's apartment to visit him. As usual I used my key to get in, but the door was stuck. I yelled for Pop to get the newspaper away from the door. I tried pushing a little harder and yelled for him again. I opened the door a few inches, just enough to try to remove the newspaper, but instead of grabbing the paper, I felt his cold, blue and bruised body. He must have fallen down, tried to get up, then fallen again.

Pop was cremated. I brought his ashes back to Syracuse and we placed his urn in the grave next to Mom. While I was there I visited all the graves of the Corso's and the Colellas, and yes including grandpa Colella, Uncle Victor and Uncle Billy.

I still think about Mom and Pop. Despite all our disagreements, and everything that happened to Joanie and to me, I miss them.

Chapter 56

I never received any awards for teaching or coaching. And that's okay. I never had time to join biology associations, or get any kind of recognition as teacher of the week, month or year. As the only wage earner in the family, I sometimes worked three jobs just to make ends meet and help my kids through college. If you're a teacher and coach, you're in it for the love of the job, not for the money.

But there are three grocery sacks of cards, letters and notes I saved from my former students starting in January of 1968 at North Arvada Junior through Bear Creek High, and finally at Arvada High. I've read them all many times. I couldn't even begin to list the names of all the students who sent me these mementos, but one letter, sums up my teaching career. It was written by Justin Oldham, a former student, who was asked by my principal to write his description of my class. It was given to me on the day of my retirement.

To the Retirement Committee:

Every day was a new adventure in Mr. Corso's class, whether it was cut and dry Biology I or his laid back approach in Biology II.

Mr. Corso did not control his students with fear. He controlled them with respect. A fun and playful teacher, he had a great sense of humor and his students really thrived on that. His antics included speaking in Klingon, from his Klingon book, threatening to fight all the boys who were not nice to girls, and showing off his "tie of the day" from his collection of 275.

He had certain rules which he established on the first day of class: Do not make fun of his hair, his weird outfits, his ties, and most important, his singing. We were allowed to listen to music, but only KVOD classical music. He kiddingly said it would raise our I.Q. a half point.

Though Mr. Corso was a fun and lively teacher, his class was no piece of cake. Many students learned this after the first test. Biology is a tough subject and he expected the students to study hard and learn the material. He is a very demanding teacher because he knows the students can do the work, if they want to. When the final grades come out, you know you earned yours and can be proud of your grade.

Mr. Corso is the ideal teacher. He caters to the needs of the students and the school because each student leaves the year with an understanding of biology.

Sincerely,

Justin Oldham.

Chapter 57

In 2000, two years after I retired from teaching, nominated by my old friend Steve Morgan, I was inducted into the Saranac Lake High School Athletic Hall of Fame. It was a great honor and one that I will always cherish. Sitting there in the auditorium waiting to make my acceptance speech, I had the same emotions I did when I graduated from high school and the University of Northern Colorado. But, as always, no one from the family was in the audience. I wish Mom and Pop could have been there to see me accept this award. And, if it was God's will, I would like to think they were watching me from heaven.

That's my story, Bunk. I really do believe that any student can achieve and succeed. Roma Towne, my wonderful teacher and friend of fifty years, must have believed it about me, even from the first day of special education class, when she came to sit beside me as I hid my head under my desk, and we both cried. A few years ago Roma wrote me a letter, and in it she said:

> You can't imagine how proud I am of you and what you have accomplished, let alone the struggles you encountered on your way, on your journey in life.
>
> From the day you told me of your accomplishments, until the day I retired, I would always tell my classes that two of the greatest highlights in my life were shaking hands with Dr. Martin Luther King and my pride in Jimmy Corso, in his drive and quest to be the best.

And actually, I'm quite proud of having had to take the hard road. Once I got to college, I did the same assignments and took the same tests as all the other students. I was never in a remedial program, took no special tests, had no special treatment. Nothing was given to me. I asked for nothing. I got what I earned, good or bad. I made the most of my situation and, with little outside help, stayed focused on my goals.

In my teaching career, I worked hard as a teacher and coach. I'm proud of my work. I took my lumps, right or wrong, but again I made no excuses. That's the way it should be.

Paisan

———————————————

About the Author

Jimmy Corso was born to Italian-American parents in 1940 in Syracuse, New York. His family life was chaotic, and before he was 15, Jimmy had attended ten different schools in Syracuse, Oswego, and finally Saranac Lake, New York. He graduated from Saranac High School in 1961.

Jimmy attended Paul Smith's Junior College from 1961 to 1963. In 1963, he enrolled at the University of Northern Colorado in Greeley, Colo, and in 1967 he earned a Bachelor's degree in Biology. He completed his Master's degree in Science Education in 1972.

In 1967 he married his college sweetheart Karren. Their two children are son Darren and daughter Kelley.

Jimmy taught biology and coached athletics at North Arvada Junior High School, Bear Creek High School, and Arvada High School. In 1997, after 30 years of teaching, Jimmy retired from the Jefferson County School District. Today he lives with his wife Karren in Arvada, Colorado, and enjoys spending time with his grandchildren.

About the Co-Author

Luanne S. Pendorf grew up in the mountains of northern New Mexico. She received both her B.A. and M.A. from the University of New Mexico. She taught high school English for 30 years in Oregon, England and Colorado. Luanne, her husband Phil, and their cats Norma and Duke split their retired time between Colorado and West Texas.

Printed in the United States
28858LVS00013B/19-27

9 781420 835595